GOODNIGHT, SLEEP TIGHT!

Six delightful quilts (and a cute do in Moda fabrics, to stitch for a special baby or child

GW00729112

*by Mimi Hollenbaugh
and Jo Baddeley*

PUDDLEDUCKS PUBLICATIONS

Goodnight, Sleep Tight!

First published in 2011 by Teamwork Craftbooks
under the imprint 'Puddleducks Publications'

Puddleducks, 116 St John's Hill, Sevenoaks, Kent, TN13 3PD
www.puddleducksquilts.co.uk

Text, photographs and quilt designs
© Jo Baddeley and © Mimi Hollenbaugh
Illustrations © Gail Lawther

ISBN 978 0 9553499 5 9
British Library Cataloguing in Publication Data
A catalogue record for this book is available from the British Library

Designed by Teamwork: Christopher & Gail Lawther
100 Wiston Avenue, Worthing, West Sussex, BN14 7PS
e-mail: thelawthers@ntlworld.com

Set in ITC Goudy Sans, Alphabet Soup & Myriad

Printed by Kenads, Goring-by-Sea, West Sussex
www.kenadsprinters.co.uk

The arrival of a child is always something to be celebrated, and what better way to do it than with a beautiful handmade quilt? We know that in these busy days, stitching time is always a luxury – and especially when you're working to a nine-month deadline; for that reason, the projects in this book are designed to be quick and easy, without losing their charm. Though the shops are full of affordable factory-made quilts and playmats, they will never match the look of a handmade one, or the love sewn into every stitch!

You will find that the delightful quilts in this book are suitable for either a boy or a girl, and can be made by hand or machine. They are small enough to finish quickly, and each one gives you a great opportunity to try colour combinations and fabrics you might not use otherwise. And just for fun, we have also included the pattern for a lovely doll, Lola – complete with her own dress and bloomers.

We hope that you enjoy both creating and giving these quilts to special little people, and we are sure that the gifts will be treasured for years to come.

Jo has designed *Baby Charms, Lollipop Stars* and *Rainbow Stars*.

Mimi has designed *ABC Quilt, Petals and Pinwheels, Piggy in the Middle,* and *Lola*

(watch out too for the next book from Puddleducks Publications, which will feature Lola's twin brother Luke!)

CONTENTS

THE PROJECTS

SEWING BASICS

EQUIPMENT

Quilting has come a long way in the past few years and there are many short-cut and alternative items available for use. However, below is a list of the basic items that you will need to make the quilts in this book, and then a list of those items that would be nice to have – things that can make certain processes easier.

Basics

❋ sewing machine, plus: assorted machine needles and ¼in foot

❋ iron and ironing board

❋ a selection of scissors: large, sharp scissors for fabric; a pair for paper and card; and embroidery scissors (small, sharp-pointed ones) for trimming points, appliqué and cutting off loose threads

❋ rotary cutting tools: rotary cutter, self-healing cutting mat with grid lines, rotary ruler (a 6 x 24in ruler is best for cutting long strips)

❋ 100% cotton fabric

❋ cotton thread

❋ needles: package of betweens (for hand quilting), size Nos 8-12; embroidery needles (for appliqué projects), assorted sizes

❋ pins (both regular sewing pins and appliqué pins for appliqué projects)

❋ thimble to fit the middle finger of your sewing hand

❋ marking tools: pencils, chalk markers, wash-out pens

❋ seam ripper

❋ freezer paper or template plastic

❋ light fusible webbing (for appliqué projects)

Additional useful items

❋ graph paper

❋ walking foot (sometimes called an even-feed foot)

❋ quilting hoop or frame for hand quilting

❋ lightbox

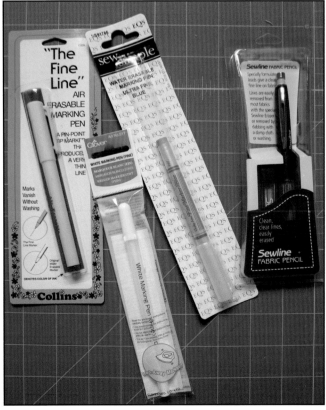

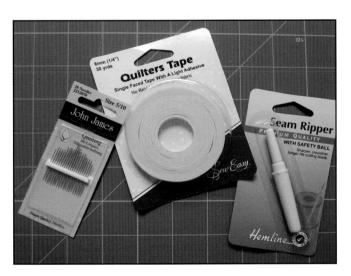

FABRICS

Selecting

Choosing the right fabrics for your quilt will determine how the quilt looks and how long it will last. Buy high-quality cotton fabric and you will enjoy working with it, your quilt will make up well, and it will look and feel wonderful. Try to avoid loose weaves and poor-quality fabric – you are going to spend many hours making your quilt, and you want it to last for years to come. Cheap cottons often fray badly, are difficult to cut and piece accurately, and are almost impossible to use successfully in needle-turn appliqué.

Most patchwork is done using cotton fabric, as it is available in thousands of prints and colours, it presses easily, and it handles well during sewing. The majority of fabrics on sale in specialised patchwork and quilting shops are 100% cotton, and generally 40-44in wide on the bolt. Wider fabrics are available in a limited range, and these are normally used for quilt backings.

Measuring

There is a definite cross-over between metric and imperial measurement in the quilting world. Because we buy fabrics in metric (metres, centimetres etc) in the UK, but in imperial (yards, inches) in the US, we will specify both in the requirements lists. However, virtually all quilting designs – and most of the quilting rulers, cutting mats etc – are based on the imperial measurements (inches), and when accurate piecing is required, it's impossible give exact conversions. Therefore, this book uses imperial measurements within the patterns themselves.

Pre-washing

Should I pre-wash my fabrics?

If your finished project is likely to be washed often (as the quilts in this book – children's quilts – are), it is advisable to pre-wash your fabrics first. This will have a two-fold benefit, both to pre-shrink your fabrics (as all cottons will shrink some amount when washed), and also to remove any excess dye from fabric that is likely to run. (Although most fabrics sold today are colour-fast, there is still the possibility of some bleed with bright fabrics – especially reds). After pre-washing, your fabrics will lose some of their sizing – the slight starchiness that makes them easier to mark and cut. If you are pre-washing, use spray starch in the ironing process to reintroduce a bit of 'body' while the fabric is still slightly damp.

Fabric terminology

Selvedges are the densely-woven finished edges of the fabric. Grain refers to the direction of the woven threads. Crosswise (weft) grain runs at right angles to the selvedges and is slightly stretchy; lengthwise (warp) grain runs parallel to the selvedges and has virtually no stretch. Bias grain runs at 45° to the selvedges and has the greatest amount of stretch.

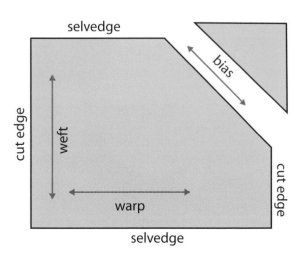

Threads

Always try to use cotton thread when sewing cotton fabric. Polyester thread is much tougher and it pulls against the cotton fibres in the fabric; over time, the cotton will wear and tear. For machine piecing, either match the thread to the fabrics in your project, or use a neutral thread such as light/medium grey.

There are many different weights and types of cotton thread available, but, as a simple rule, use a medium-weight (40) cotton for hand or machine piecing.

Silk threads are sometimes considered to be the very best for appliqué, but they do have disadvantages: they're expensive, and they slide out of the needle easily. Fine cotton thread should work well for most of your needle-turn appliqué projects. Note, though, that the thread colour should match your appliqué piece, not the background. If you cannot match the appliqué piece exactly, opt for a shade lighter rather than darker; darker threads are harder to hide.

Quilting thread is sold as either 'hand quilting thread,' or 'machine quilting/machine embroidery thread'. You can use a machine thread to quilt by hand, but not vice-versa.

☞ REMEMBER

Don't use hand quilting thread in your sewing machine; choose a specific machine quilting or machine embroidery thread.

Wadding/batting

There are many different types of wadding (batting) on the market, ranging from 2oz polyester through to cotton, silk, wool and bamboo. As with fabric, the better the quality of your wadding, the more enjoyable your project will be to quilt – and the better it will hang and wear. But, do consider how your quilt will be used: if it's for a child (as the projects in this book are), and so will be frequently washed, then a polyester wadding is probably the best choice. But if you like the slightly crinkled look of antique quilts, then choose a cotton wadding, as this is thinner and it will shrink slightly when washed. Check the packaging – this will often give you information about the suitability of the wadding for hand or machine quilting, and how much it will shrink when washed. If you decide to use a cotton or poly/cotton mix wadding, if you wish you can pre-wash it so that it's pre-shrunk before you layer it into your quilt.

Backing

The backing fabric for your quilt should be 100% cotton. The piece of fabric for the backing needs to be at least 2in larger on all sides than the quilt top, as the quilt top may move and stretch slightly as you quilt. If you need to join lengths of fabric to make the backing, then cut off the selvedges and open out the seam to reduce bulk. Press the entire piece of backing fabric before you layer the quilt (see page 59).

GENERAL NOTES

If you are new to quilting, you'll find the sewing techniques that you need to make the projects in this book explained clearly on pages 46-63. If you're already an experienced quilter, you almost certainly already know the techniques required, but the information is there at the back of the book if there's something you're not sure of, or if you want a little reminder!

Quilt materials shown used in this book are NOT fire retardant.

Buttons on quilts are not suitable for those under three years of age.

BABY CHARMS

Any baby would be delighted with this quick and easy quilt – its cheerful colours are ideal for tucking round a toddler in a buggy, or for snuggling under while you read a favourite story.

Finished size 35 x 47in (90 x 120cm)

You will need:

❀ one charm pack containing at least 36 5in squares *(I used Moda Hideaway Charm Pack)*

❀ 1¼yd (1.2m) background fabric

❀ 18in (40cm) for the inner border and binding

❀ 40 x 55in (100 x 130cm) piece of wadding

Preparation

Planning your design

Select 24 squares (we'll call these A squares) from the charm pack – ones with large-print designs are particularly good. Set them out in a 4 x 6 pattern as shown (**a**), with a good mix of colours and tones across the design. Choose 12 more squares, preferably ones with small prints, for the border (B squares).

a

Cutting

1 From the background fabric, cut:
– 11 strips measuring 2in x the width of the fabric
– 4 strips measuring 1½in x the width of the fabric
– 48 pieces measuring 2 x 4½in

From the offcuts of the final step above, cut four 2in squares

2 From the inner border/binding fabric, cut:
– 4 strips measuring 1in x the width of the fabric
– 4 strips measuring 2½in x the width of the fabric

Making the quilt top

Note: use ¼in seams throughout

Creating the centre design

3 Sew one of the 2 x 4½in background strips to the left-hand side of every A square (**b**). Sew the A squares together in six rows of four squares, keeping the layout you chose for the A blocks, then sew another 2 x 4½in background strip to the right-hand end of every row (**c**).

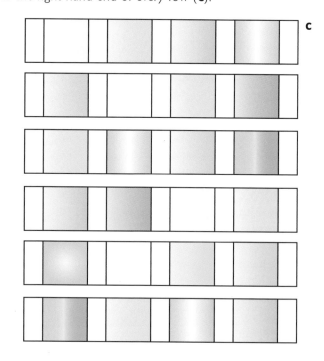

c

4 Measure the length of these rows, and cut seven of the 2in background strips to this measurement; stitch one of these to the top of each row of squares (**d**), and

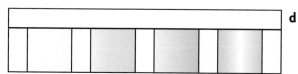

d

sew the final one to the bottom of the final row of squares. Sew the rows together, taking care to line up the squares in each row (**e**).

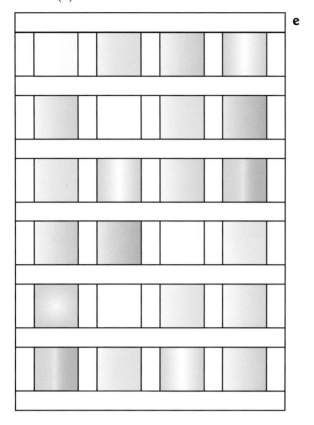

e

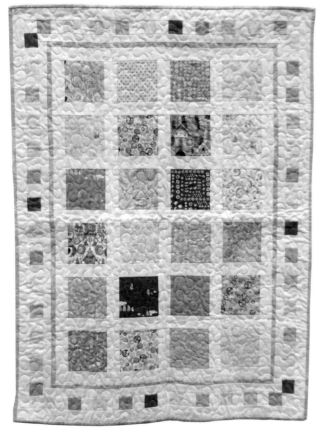

Adding the inner borders

5 Measure the size of the quilt top; it should measure approximately 26 x 38in. Cut two of the 1in border strips to the width of the quilt, and sew these to the top and bottom of the quilt. Remeasure the length of the quilt; cut the other two border strips to this length, and sew them to the sides of the quilt. Repeat this process with the 1½in background strips (**f**).

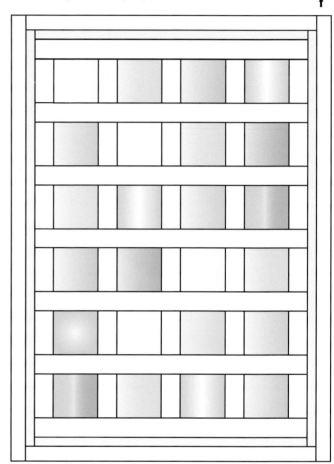

f

Adding the outer borders

6 Take the 12 patterned squares you have chosen for the border. From each one cut two rectangles (**g**), each measuring 5 x 2in (you will have a 1in strip left over from each square); you now have 24 rectangles. Sew a background 2 x 4½in piece to one long side of each rectangle (**h**). Cut each of these blocks in half horizontally to make two rectangles, each measuring 3½ x 2in (**i**).

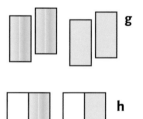

g

h

i

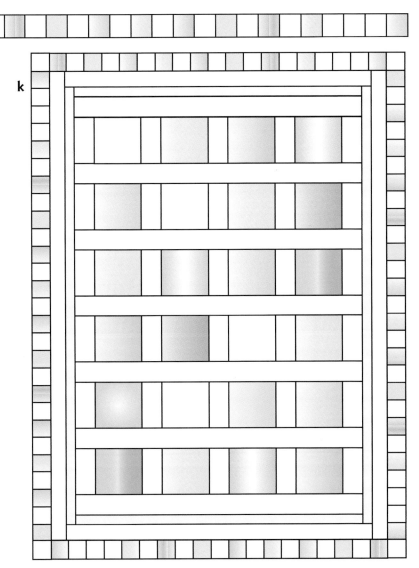

7 Sew ten of these rectangles together, alternating the background and patterned squares (**j**). Unstitch and remove the background square at the end of the row, then sew this row of squares to the top of the quilt. Repeat with another row of squares at the bottom of the quilt.

8 Take 14 of the border rectangles and sew them together in the same way, adding an extra background square at the end of the row. Sew this to the side of the quilt, then repeat the process for the other side (**k**).

9 Remeasure the quilt top. Cut two of the 2in background strips to the width of the quilt and sew these to the top and bottom of the design. Cut the other two 2in background strips to the length of the quilt, and sew them to the sides to complete the quilt top (**l**).

Finishing

10 Quilt as desired, by hand or machine. Sew the 2½in binding strips together and press them in half lengthways (wrong sides together); use this strip to bind the quilt (see page 62) as shown (**m**).

l

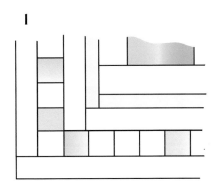

m

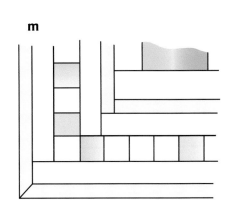

This bright and cheerful quilt is perfect for those occasions when you don't know the gender of the coming baby, and/or you want a project that is quick to make up!

Finished size 42 x 54in (107 x 137cm)

You will need:

(the details in brackets are the fabrics that I used)

❀ 1¾yd (1.6m) yellow fabric for the background *(Moda Essential Dots Yellow 8654-20)*

❀ ¼yd (25cm) each of the following for the appliqué
green *(Moda Marble Stars 3406-106 Lime)*
pink *(Moda Puzzle Pieces Specks 1004-32 Pink)*
dark blue *(Moda Marble Stars 3406-103 Bright Blue)*
light blue *(Moda Marble Stars 3406-55 Sky Blue)*
red *(Moda Marble Stars 3406-32 Red)*
purple *(Moda Marble Mate Dots 3405-20 Lavender)*

❀ scraps of dark blue, dark green and red for the appliqué crayons

❀ embroidery floss or machine-sewing threads to match your appliqué fabrics (depending on whether you want to hand-stitch or machine-stitch around the appliqué patches)

❀ 45 x 60in (115 x 152cm) piece of wadding

❀ 1½yd (1.5m) fabric for the backing

❀ fusible webbing (or template plastic/tracing paper and card for creating the templates, if you are doing needle-turn appliqué instead of fused appliqué)

Preparation

Cutting

1 For the appliqué block backgrounds, cut nine 9 x 13in rectangles of the yellow fabric (the most economical way to do this is to cut three 9in strips x the width of the fabric, then sub-cut each of these into three 13in rectangles).

2 For the inside and outside borders, cut nine 3½in strips x the width of the yellow fabric. For the middle border, cut nine 3½in squares of each of the six appliqué fabrics (green, pink, dark blue, light blue, red and purple), to give you a total of 54 squares.

Doing the appliqué

3 Trace templates A-F onto fusible webbing, and cut the shapes out roughly (see the instructions for fusible web appliqué on page 53 for more details of the method). Iron each shape onto the wrong side of the appropriate appliqué fabric, then cut the shapes out along the marked lines (**a**).

a

4 Lay six of the yellow background rectangles on a flat surface so that the long edges are vertical, then peel off the paper backings of the appliqué shapes and iron one letter or number onto each yellow patch (**b**).

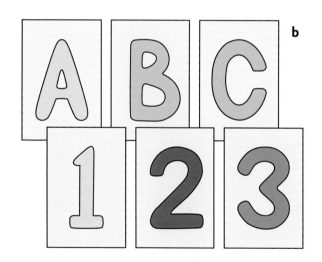
b

5 Use the same method to prepare appliqué shapes for the apple, stalk and leaf (using templates G-I), two balloons (trace template J twice), and three crayons (trace templates K and L three times each). Lay the final three yellow rectangles out so that the long edges are vertical, and fuse the apple, stem and leaf onto the centre of the first rectangle (**c**). Fuse the balloons onto the upper portion of the second rectangle (**d**),

c

d

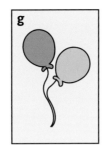

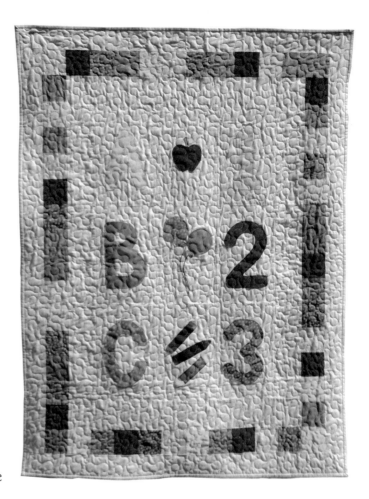

then scatter the three crayons centrally in the third rectangle, applying the basic crayon shapes first (**e**) and then the rectangular patches on top (**f**).

6 On each rectangle, stitch around the edges of the appliqué pieces using either a sewing machine (satin stitch or other decorative stitch), or by hand using blanket stitch and two strands of matching embroidery floss. Embroider strings for the balloons using backstitch and two strands of black embroidery floss (**g**).

Making the quilt top

Note: use ¼in seams throughout

7 Trim the appliqué blocks to 8½ x 12½in, and stitch them together in the design shown (**h**). On each side of the design, stitch a 3½in strip of yellow fabric, trimming the strips to length. Use the same method to add two more strips of yellow to the top and bottom (**i**).

8 Randomly sew together two sets of fourteen 3½in coloured squares and add these borders to the sides of the quilt top (**j**); for the top and bottom, stitch two sets of

twelve 3½in squares and add them in the same way (**k**). (Note: you will have two small squares left over from the 54 you originally cut.)

h

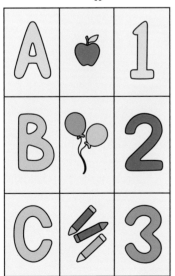

i

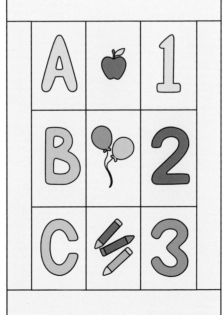

j

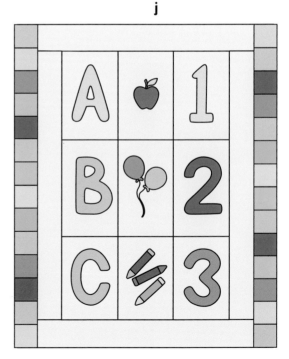

9 Piece together three of the remaining strips of yellow fabric, then re-cut them to give you two 48½ x 3½in strips; sew these to the sides of the quilt. Add the final two yellow strips to the top and bottom of the quilt.

Finishing

10 Layer the quilt top with the wadding and backing, and quilt by hand or machine; bind as desired!

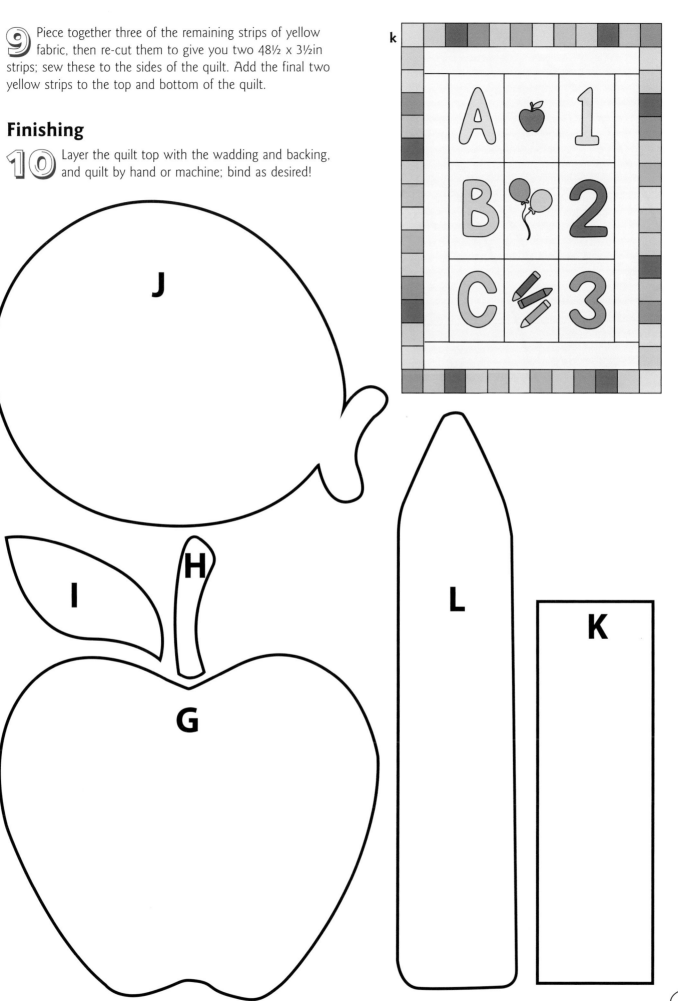

A

B

C

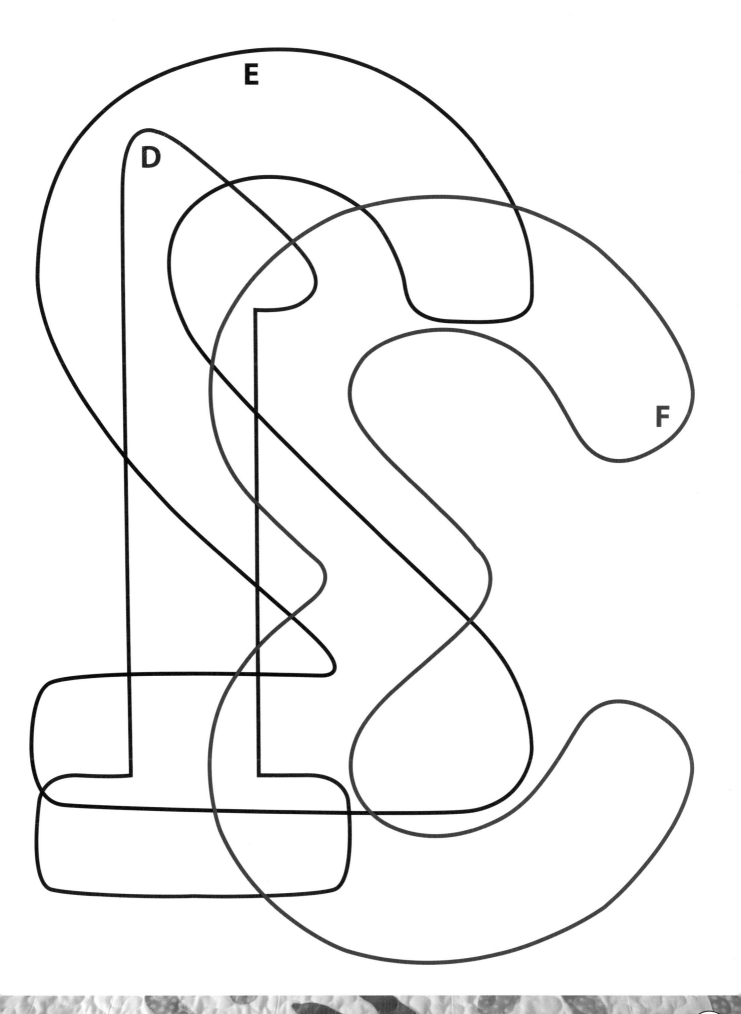

Choose fabrics with lots of interest for this playmat – can you find the fishes and alphabet letters?

Finished size 44in (112cm) square

You will need:

(the details in brackets are the fabrics that I used)

❋ one charm pack containing at least 42 5in squares (Moda Lollipop Charm Pack)

❋ 1yd (1m) cream-on-cream or white-on-white print fabric

❋ 24in (60cm) fabric for the border (Moda Lollipop 17555-11)

❋ 2½yd (2.5m) 42-44in wide backing fabric, or use 1¼yd (1.25m) and add strips of contrast fabric to the selvedges to increase the width to approx 50in

❋ approx 50in (127cm) square of wadding

❋ 12in (35cm) fabric for the binding (Moda Lollipop 17559-16)

Preparation

Choosing your colours

Sort the charm pack into the colours for the four star blocks. Ideally, you need:

• four sets of patches, each set containing four squares in a similar colour (in our sample we used four squares each of green, yellow, red and blue). For easy reference we will call these A squares.

• four squares of a contrast colour (in our sample, brown); these are B squares.

• eight squares of a relatively neutral colour (in our sample, cream patterns); cut these squares down to 4½in. These are C squares.

• eight squares of random colours; these are D squares.

Cutting

From the cream or white print fabric fabric, cut:
- twenty-eight 5in squares (these are E squares)
- four strips, each measuring 2½in x the width of the fabric.

From the border fabric, cut:
- five strips each measuring 4½in x the width of the fabric

Making up the quilt

Creating the star blocks

1 Draw a diagonal line on the back of each A, B and D square (**a**). Pair up each of these squares with a white or cream E square, and place the squares right sides together; follow the instructions on page 48 to create a series of squares consisting of half-square triangles (**b**). Trim each one up so that it measures 4½in square.

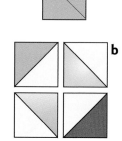
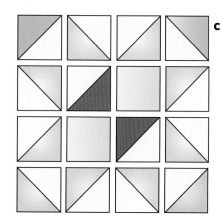

2 Take eight of these new patches made from the A squares in a single colour (eg green). Now take two of the B squares (pick ones that feature the same contrast print), two of the neutral C squares, and four random patches made from D squares. Lay these patches out in a 4 x 4 design as shown (**c**).

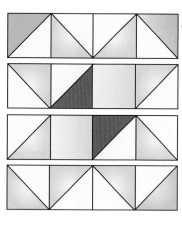

3 Join the patches together in four rows as shown (**d**), then join the rows to complete the star block (**e**).

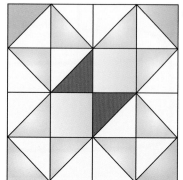

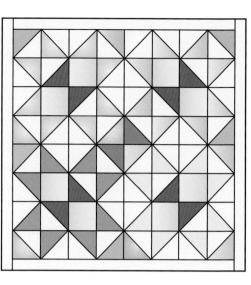

6 Use the same method to add strips of border fabric to create the wide border (**h**); cut one of the border strips in half and join each half to one of the other strips – use these for the longer sides.

4 Make the other three star blocks in the same way, and join them to create the centre of the quilt top (**f**).

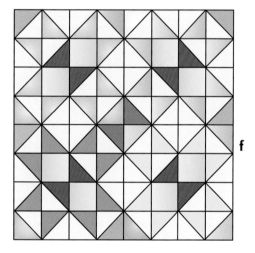

f

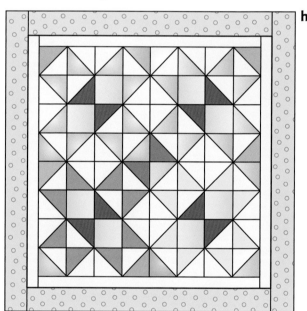

h

Adding the borders

5 Measure the design (it should measure 32½in square). Cut two of the wide cream/white strips to this measured length, and sew them to the top and bottom of the quilt; measure again, cut the other two strips to this length, and add them to the sides of the quilt (**g**).

Finishing

7 Layer the quilt top with the backing and wadding and quilt as you wish by hand or machine. Trim the quilt square if necessary, then cut the binding fabric into 2½in strips; join these into one long length and press the strip along its length, wrong sides together; follow the instructions on page 62 to bind the edges of the quilt.

PETALS & PINWHEELS QUILT

The pinwheels seem to spin around the bright flowers of this quilt.

Finished size 58in (147cm) square

You will need:

(the details in brackets are the fabrics that I used)

❀ 2yd (2m) white for the background (Moda Muslin Mates 9920-11)

❀ ¾yd (75cm) floral print for the appliqué flowers (Moda Dilly Dally 22141-13)

❀ ½yd (50cm) pink for the appliqué flower centres and second border (Moda Dilly Dally 22145-15)

❀ ¾yd (75cm) teal for the pinwheels (Moda Dilly Dally 22146-14)

❀ 1yd (1m) blue for the first and third borders (Moda Dilly Dally 22144-23)

❀ ½yd (50cm) floral print for binding (Moda Dilly Dally 22144-23)

❀ 61in (155cm) square piece of wadding

❀ 3½yd (3.25m) fabric for backing

❀ pencil, plus template plastic or tracing paper and card, for making the appliqué templates

Preparation

For the appliqué blocks

1 From the white fabric, cut thirteen 10in squares for the flower background.

2 Trace and cut out template A, and use this to cut out thirteen flowers; this template doesn't include any extra for the seams, so add ¼in seam allowances as you cut out the shapes if you are doing needle-turn appliqué.

3 Trace and cut out template B, and use this to cut out thirteen flower centres (again, remember to add seam allowances if necessary when cutting).

For the pinwheel blocks

4 From the white fabric cut:
– twenty-four 5³⁄₈in squares
– forty-eight 2¼in squares
From the teal fabric cut:
– twenty-four 5³⁄₈in squares

For the borders

5 From the blue fabric cut:
– five 2in strips x the width of the fabric for the first border
– six 3½in strips x the width of the fabric for the third border
From the pink fabric cut:
– five 2in strips x the width of the fabric for the second border

Appliqué

6 Using either needle-turn or fusible web appliqué (see page 53), appliqué the thirteen flower blocks. Find the centre of each square of background fabric, and line this up with the centre point of the flower. Pin the flower to the background and sew around the edge (**a**). Centre the pink circles on the flowers and sew around the edges (**b**). Trim the appliqué blocks to 9½in square.

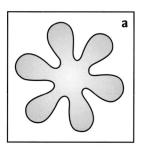

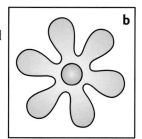

Making the pinwheel blocks

 On the wrong side of each of the large and small white squares, draw a diagonal line in pencil (**c**). Pair each of the large white squares with a teal square, right sides together, and stitch a seam ¼in each side of the drawn line (**d**). Cut along the pencil lines (**e**), and press the seams towards the dark fabric; you will now have forty-eight 5in squares (**f**).

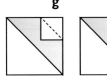

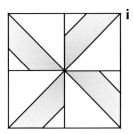

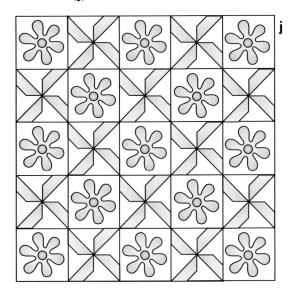 On the teal corner of each block, pin a 2¼in white square, right sides together, and stitch on the drawn line (**g**). Clip off the spare fabric at the corner and press the seam towards the light fabric (**h**).

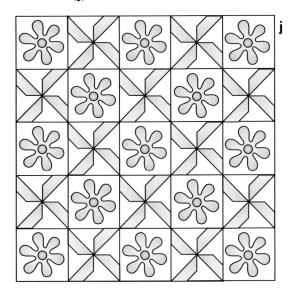 Stitch four of these pieced squares together as shown to make a pinwheel block (**i**); create twelve blocks this way, making sure that the pinwheels all spin in the same direction.

Making the quilt top

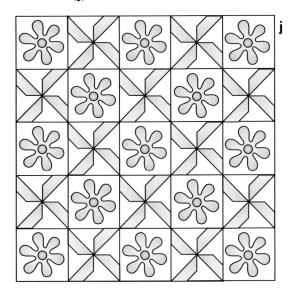 Join the appliquéd flower blocks and the pinwheel blocks together alternately in the pattern shown (**j**).

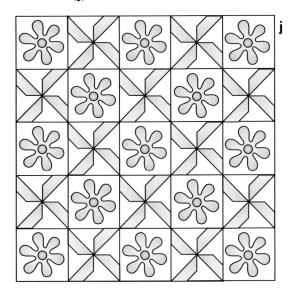

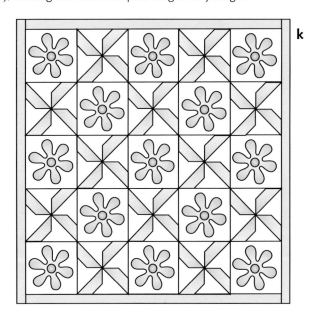 To make the borders:
• Join the five 2in blue strips to make one long strip, then use this to stitch borders first of all to the top and bottom of the quilt, and then to the left and right sides (**k**), cutting the fabric strip to length as you go.

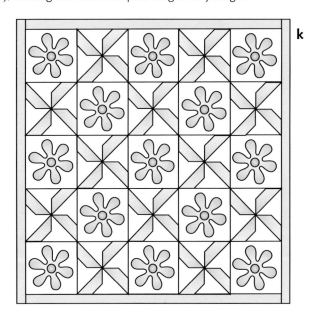

• Join the five 2in pink strips to make one long strip, then use the same method to add these borders to the quilt (**l**).

• Join the six 3½in blue strips to make one long strip, then use the same method to add these borders to the quilt (diagram **m** overleaf).

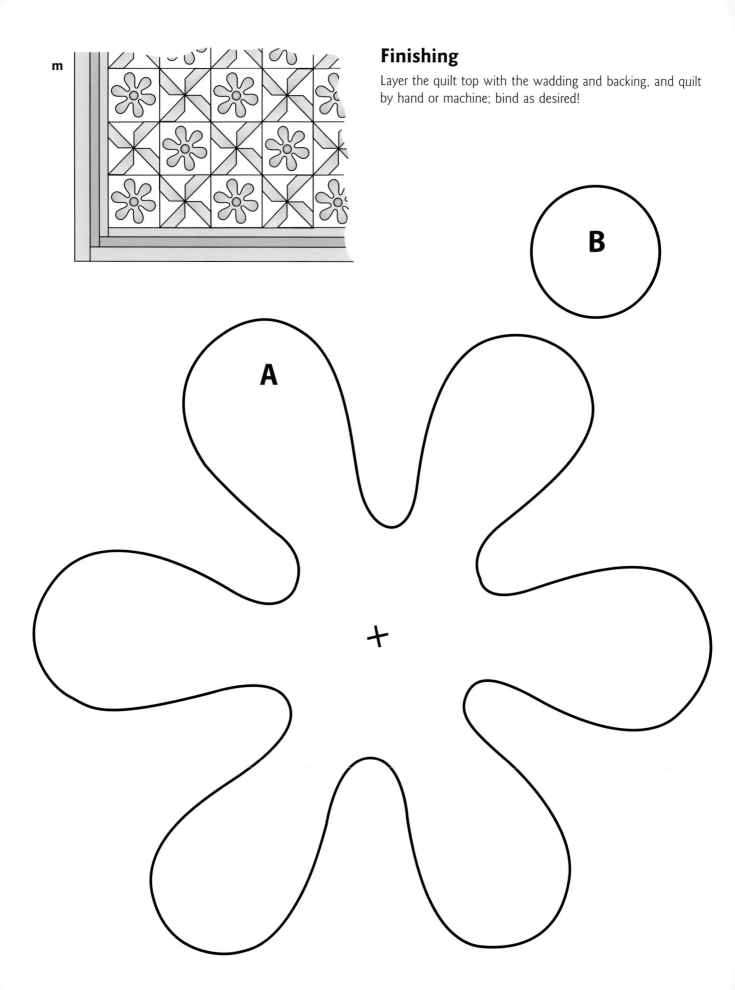

m

Finishing

Layer the quilt top with the wadding and backing, and quilt by hand or machine; bind as desired!

B

A

+

Babies usually love primary colours and bold shapes – so this bright quilt will be fun for playtime.

Finished size 28 x 42in (72 x 107cm)

You will need:

(the details in brackets are the fabrics that I used)

- ❀ nine fat eighths of brightly-coloured fabrics *(Moda Essential Dots)*
- ❀ 1yd (1m) white-on-white or plain white fabric
- ❀ ½yd (50cm) sashing fabric *(Moda Essential Dots Navy 8654-25)*
- ❀ 10in (30cm) binding fabric *(Moda Essential Dots Sunshine 8654-37) (or use offcuts from the fat eighths)*
- ❀ 1½yd (1.5m) backing fabric *(Moda Dottie White/Teal 45008-25)*
- ❀ 36 x 48in (92 x 120cm) piece of wadding

Making the star blocks

Cutting

1 From six of the bright fabrics cut one 4½in square (**a**); these are A squares, and will be used in the centres of the stars.

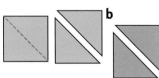

2 From each of the nine bright fabrics, cut a 4⅞in square; cut these squares along one diagonal to give you 18 triangles (**b**). From the three bright fabrics that were not used for the centre squares, cut another 4⅞in square and cut along one diagonal to create another six triangles. You will now have a total of 24 large triangles; we'll call these the B triangles.

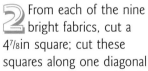

3 From each of the nine bright fabrics, cut two 5¼in squares and cut along both diagonals (**c**) to produce 36 small C triangles.

4 From the white background fabric, cut twenty-four 4½in squares, and six 5¼in squares. Cut the 5¼in squares along both diagonals to give a further twenty-four small C triangles.

Piecing the blocks
Note: use ¼in seams throughout

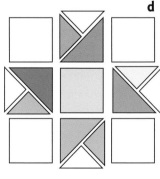

5 Using a good mix of colours, lay out a Rainbow Star block as shown (**d**). Sew the white C triangles to the small coloured C triangles (**e**).

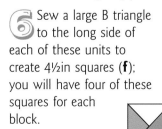

6 Sew a large B triangle to the long side of each of these units to create 4½in squares (**f**); you will have four of these squares for each block.

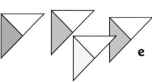

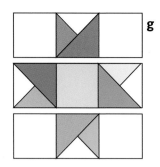

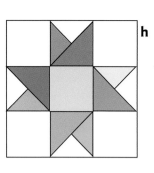

7 Lay the block out in order again, and seam the squares together in three rows of three (**g**), then join the rows to create the finished block (**h**). Repeat this process to make six different star blocks (you will have some spare small coloured triangles left over). Square up and trim the star blocks to 12½in square.

Making the quilt top

8 From the sashing fabric, cut six strips each 2in wide x the width of the fabric (44in). Sub-cut these strips to give you eighteen strips measuring 12½ x 2in.

9 From the nine bright fabrics, cut twelve 2in squares. Make a sashing row by joining three of these squares with two of the sashing strips as shown (**i**); make four strips this way.

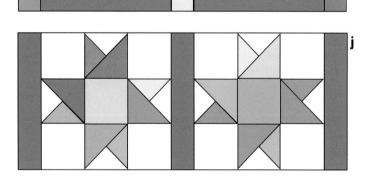

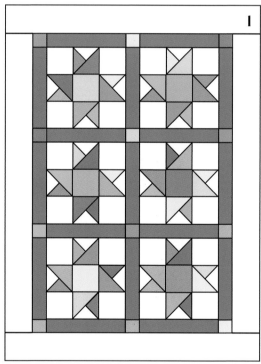

10 Join three of the sashing strips with two star blocks as shown (**j**); make three rows this way, then join the rows of blocks and sashing to make the quilt top (**k**).

11 From the white fabric, cut four strips each 3in wide x the width of the fabric. Sew two of these to the sides of the quilt top, and trim to fit; sew the other two strips to the top and bottom of the quilt, and trim to fit (**l**).

Finishing

12 Layer the quilt with the wadding and the backing, and quilt as desired by hand or machine. Cut the binding fabric into 2½in wide strips, join the strips, and use this piece to bind the quilt (see page 62).

A fun farm animal quilt to make for either a boy or a girl!

Finished size 49 x 48in (125 x 122cm)

You will need:

(the details in brackets are the fabrics that I used)

- ¼yd (20cm) white/green print fabric for the sheep (Moda Dottie 45008-23)
- ¼yd (20cm) white/black print fabric for the cows (Moda Dottie 45008-17)
- ¼yd (20cm) or 8in (20cm) square scrap of white/pink print for the pig (Moda Dottie 45008-29)
- scraps of grey, green and pink for the animals' heads and feet
- 2yd (1.75m) green for the grass (Moda Marble Dots 3405-106 Lime)
- ¾yd (75cm) brown for the fence (Moda Puzzle Pieces 1008-41)
- ½yd (50cm) fabric for the binding (Moda Marble Dots 3405-106 Lime)
- 49 x 52in piece of wadding
- 2¾yd (2.5m) fabric for the backing
- template plastic, or tracing paper and card, for creating the appliqué templates

Cutting

For the appliqué blocks

1. Cut nine 10½ x 13½in rectangles of the grass fabric for the sheep background (note: the most economical way to do this is to cut three 10½in strips x the width of the fabric, then sub-cut each of these into three 13½in rectangles).

2. Trace templates A-J onto card or template plastic, and cut out. Using template A, cut out four sheep shapes from the sheep fabric (**a**); if you're doing needle-turn appliqué, add ¼in seam allowance all

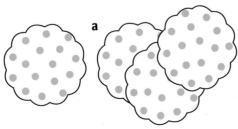

the way around all the animal pieces as you're cutting them out, as shown in the photographs below – if you are using raw-edge appliqué, you don't need to add seam allowances. Use template B to cut four sheep heads from the appropriate fabric, and template C to cut eight sheep feet (**b**).

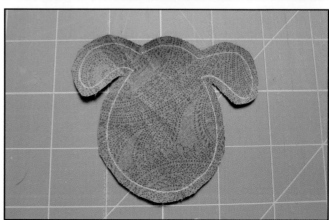

3 In the same way, use template D to cut four cow shapes from the cow fabric (**c**), then template E to cut four cow heads; use template C again to cut 16 cow feet (**d**).

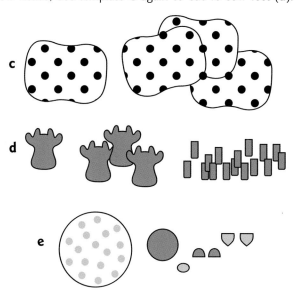

4 Finally, use template F to cut one pig body, template G to cut one pig head, template H to cut one pig snout, template I to cut two pig feet, and template J to cut two pig ears (**e**).

For the fence border

5 From the green fabric cut nine strips, 2½in wide x the width of fabric, then from these strips cut:

– two 27½ x 2½in strips
– twelve 5½ x 2½in patches.

Put aside the remaining five strips for the outside border.

6 Still working with the green fabric, cut two strips 5½in wide x the width of fabric, then sub-cut these strips into twelve 5½in squares.

7 From the brown fabric cut eight strips 2½in wide x the width of fabric, then from these strips cut:

– twelve 5½ x 2½in patches
– ten 9½ x 2½in strips.

Put aside the remaining three strips for the outside border.

Appliqué

8 Using either needle-turn or fusible web appliqué (as detailed in the instructions starting on page 53), appliqué the four sheep, four cows and one pig onto the green background fabric:

- Find the centre of each rectangle of background fabric, and line this up with the centre point of the animal body pattern; lightly pin the body to the background (**f**).

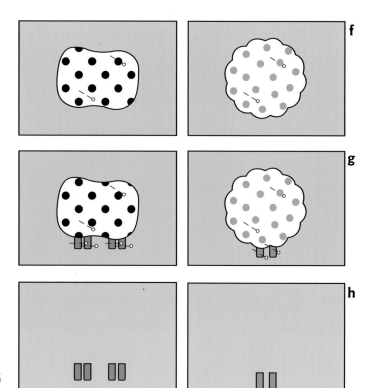

- Using the templates as a guide, pin the legs of the sheep and cows in place, as shown in **g**. Unpin the body and sew the feet to the background (**h**).
- Return the body patch to the background fabric, matching the centre points, and sew around the shape (**i**).

- Pin the head to the body, using the template as a guide to positioning, and sew around the shape (**j**); remember to do two cows facing one way, and two facing the other way.
- To appliqué the pig, attach the body patch first (**k**) and then sew on (in this order) the face, snout, ears and feet (**l**).

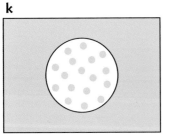

k

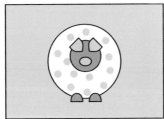

l

o

Making the quilt top

Note: use ¼in seams throughout

9 Trim the blocks to 9½ x 12½in, and stitch them together as shown (**m**); the four cows go in the corners, the sheep in the centre of each side, and the piggy in the middle (obviously!) Stitch the two 27½x 2½in strips of green to each side of this design (**n**).

10 Make twelve fence rail blocks by taking a 5½in green square and sewing a 2½ x 5½in brown strip on top, then a 2½ x 5½in green strip on top of that (**o**).

11 Take six of the fence rail blocks; join them with a 2½ x 9½in brown strip (fence posts) in between, turning every second rail block the other way up so that the rails alternate as shown (**p**). Join the remaining six rail blocks and fence posts in the same way, but this time with the starting rail in the top position as shown (**q**). Sew these fence sections to the top and bottom of the quilt (**r**).

m

n

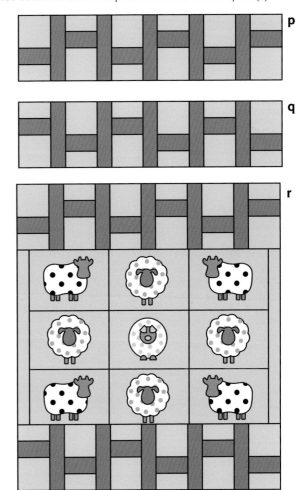

p

q

r

12 To make the outside borders, take the three long 2½in brown strips you put aside earlier and join them into one long strip. From this, cut two pieces each 45½in long, and sew to the left and right sides of the quilt (**s**). Now take the five long 2½in green strips and join them into one long strip. From this, cut two pieces each 45½in long and sew to the sides, then cut two pieces each 48½in long and sew to the top and bottom (**t**).

Finishing

Layer the quilt top with the wadding and backing, and quilt as you wish by hand or machine; bind as desired!

s

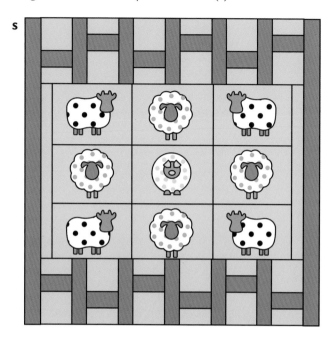

t

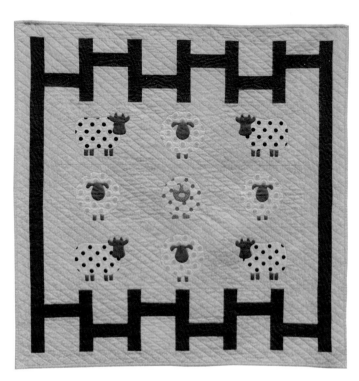

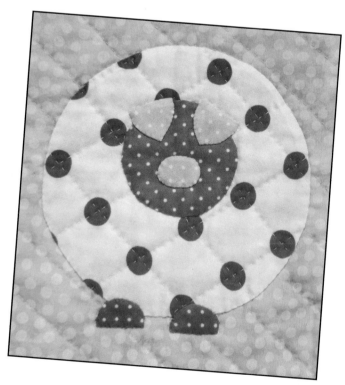

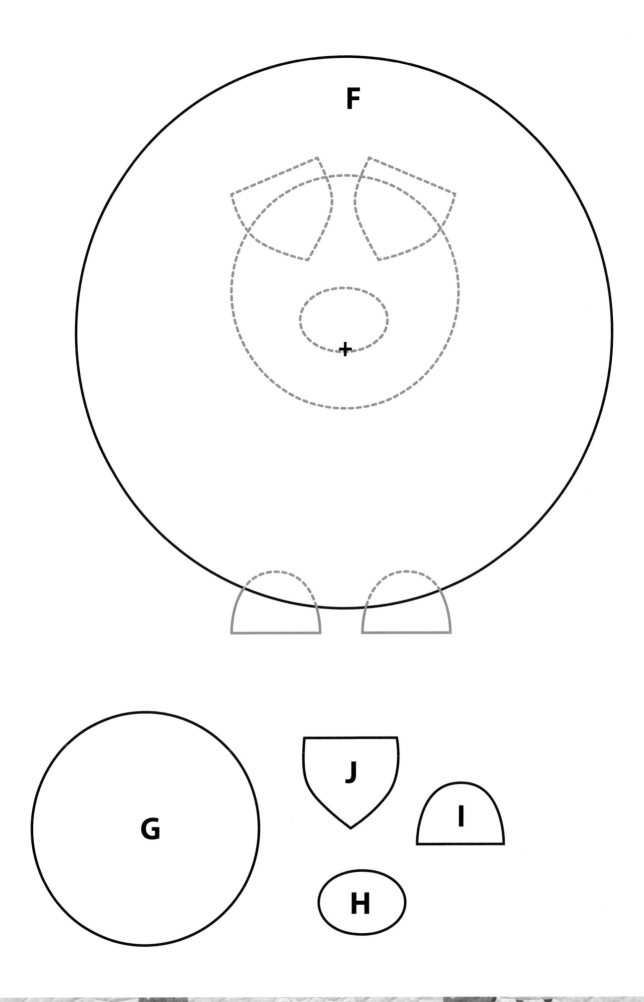

F

G

J

I

H

A

+

C

B

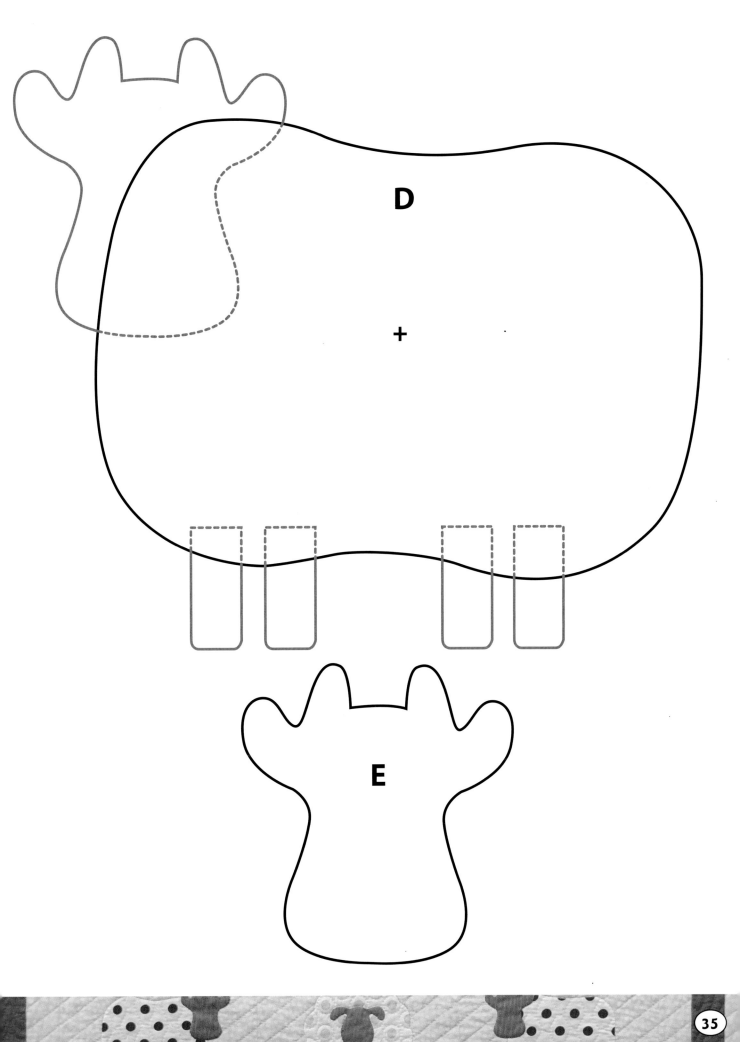

D

E

Lola is a fun and easy-to-make doll; she would be a nice gift for someone special in your life, or for you to enjoy yourself.

Finished size approximately 20in (50cm) tall

You will need:

(the details in brackets are the fabrics that I used)

❋ ½yd (40cm) light-coloured fabric for the body (*Moda Marble Flag Ivory 9880-87*)

❋ ½yd (40cm) fabric for the dress (*Moda Girlie Girl 10784-12*)

❋ ¼yd (25cm) fabric for the bloomers (*Moda Basics Marble Dots Light Pink 3405-58*)

❋ 6 x 30in (15 x 76cm) piece of fleece for the hair

❋ 1yd (1m) thin elastic

❋ 1yd (1m) thin ribbon

❋ 1½yd (1.5m) narrow lace

❋ two black buttons for eyes

❋ two snaps (poppers)

❋ red and black embroidery thread

❋ toy stuffing

❋ freezer paper

❋ pencil or water-soluble pen

❋ sticky tape, fabric glue

Making the body

Note: Lola's body is made by pressing/pinning paper patterns directly onto the fabric and sewing around them, so these pattern pieces do not include a seam allowance: the seam allowance will be added when you cut the stitched shapes out, as explained in the instructions below.

1 Trace the pattern pieces for the body, arms and legs (templates A–C) onto freezer paper or thick tracing paper (trace the arm and leg pieces twice), and cut out on the lines. Join the two parts of the body pattern (A1 and A2) with sticky tape, matching the arrows.

2 Fold the body fabric in half, right sides together; position the freezer paper patterns for the legs and arms onto the fabric, shiny side down, leaving at least half

an inch between the shapes, and iron in place (**a**). (If you are using tracing paper, pin the patches securely in place, again leaving half an inch between the paper shapes.)

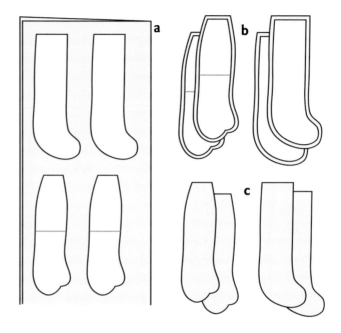

3 Stitch along the edge of the paper around the arm and leg shapes, leaving openings for turning at the tops; reinforce seams at the edges of each opening. Cut out the arm and leg shapes, leaving a ¼in seam allowance (**b**), remove the freezer paper, and turn the shapes the right way out (**c**).

4 Lay the paper pattern for the body/head on the wrong side of the body fabric and mark around the head portion with a pencil or water-soluble pen. On the right side of the fabric, trace the face from template D (the outline of the head you've drawn on the back will help you to centre the face), and embroider the mouth, nose and eyelashes on the right side of the fabric, using two strands of embroidery floss (**d**).

5 Now fold the body fabric right sides together, lay the paper head/body pattern face in position again and press/pin it in position (**e**), and sew around the outside of the pattern, leaving the bottom edge open for turning. Reinforce the opening and neck portions of the body with a second set of stitches. Remove the freezer paper, clip the curves, and turn the body right side out (**f**).

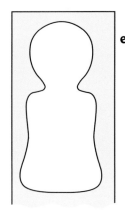

e f g

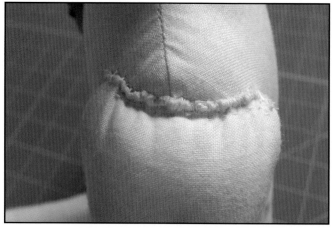

Close-up showing the hand-stitched seam joining the arm to the shoulder

6 Stuff the legs and body/head portion of the doll, and slipstitch the openings closed. (For the best results when you are attaching the feet to the body, stitch the feet so that the seams run down the centre front and back of the feet, not the sides, as shown in **g**).

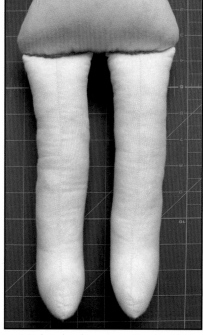

Stitch Lola's legs on so that her feet face the front

7 Sew on the eyes (**h**), stitching through the back of the head to the front; pull up the threads slightly to create small indents in Lola's face around the eyes.

8 Stuff the arms up to the line indicated on the template, as shown in the photograph below, and pin closed; machine-stitch across each arm on this line, so that Lola can later bend her arms. Stuff the rest of the arms and slipstitch the openings closed (**i**).

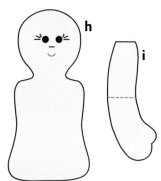

h i

9 Hand stitch the legs to the bottom of the body, and the arms to the edges of the shoulders as shown in the photograph above, making sure that the feet and arms face forwards (**j**)

j

k

Adding the hair

10 Cut out the hair piece (template E) from fleece. Hand stitch this piece of fleece to the back of the head, centring the dotted line on the top seam of the head and folding the cut-out or V portions to meet each other, as indicated by the arrows on the template. This creates a kind of cap across the back of Lola's head and high over her forehead (**k**).

11 Cut a 5 x 20in piece of fleece, orientating it so that the 5in width is with the 'stretch' of the fleece, and the 20in length not providing much stretch. (When you are cutting the head pattern piece, the orientation of the fleece does not matter.) Stitch a line by machine down the centre of this long piece of fleece to create a hair parting. Working from the outer edges towards the centre, cut strips into the fleece (**l**), being careful not to cut right into the centre!

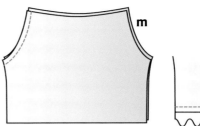
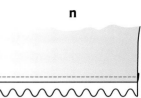

12 Centre this fleece patch on the back and top of the head, covering the 'cap' sewn on in step 10, and attach it by hand, stitching down the sewn parting line. (Make sure you stitch all the way through both layers of fleece and the head fabric.) Lay the hair flat down both sides of the head and glue the hair down just out to the edge of the head. Braid/plait the remaining length of hair on each side of the head as shown above and tie each braid with ribbon.

Making the clothes

Use ¼in seams unless otherwise indicated; on these pattern pieces, the seam allowance is included.

The bloomers

13 Cut out two pieces of fabric for the bloomers using template F. With right sides together, stitch the centre front seam (**m**). Make a waistband casing by folding over the top of the bloomers twice and topstitching. (The width of your casing will be determined by the width of your elastic – use a thin elastic, and make sure that your casing is wide enough to fit it comfortably.)

On these clothes patterns, seam allowances are already included so you don't need to add them

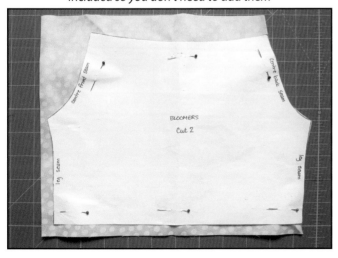

14 Cut an 8½in length of elastic and insert it into the casing using a bodkin or safety pin, securing the elastic in place with stitches at each side. Hem each of the legs by making a ¼in double fold along the bottom edge and stitching; sew lace over the top of the hem (**n**).

The inside of one bloomers leg, showing the elastic

15 Cut two 5½in lengths of elastic; sew these to the bottom of each bloomer leg, on the wrong side, 1in up from the hem,  stretching the elastic as you sew so that it extends the entire width of the fabric (**o**). Stitch the centre back of the bloomers. Lining up the centre front and centre back seams, stitch the inside leg of the bloomers.

Lola modelling the finished bloomers

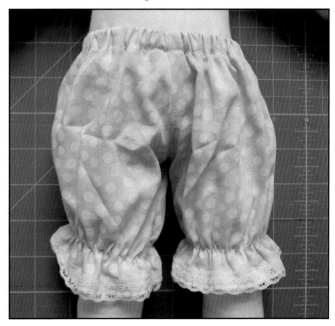

The dress

16 Cut a 10 x 30in rectangle of fabric for the skirt, and set this aside. Using templates G, H and I, cut out two back bodices, one front bodice and two sleeve pieces for the dress (**p**). With right sides together, sew the front and back bodices together at the shoulder seams (**q**).

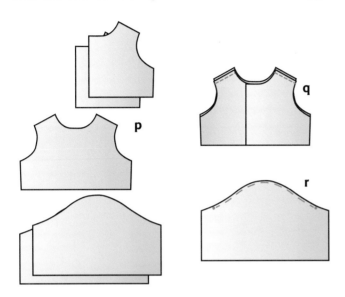

17 Run a gathering thread between the dots at the top of each sleeve (**r**), gather the edges to fit the armholes, and sew the sleeves to the armhole openings (**s**). Hem each of the sleeves by making a ¼in double fold along the bottom edge. Sew lace over the top of the hem.

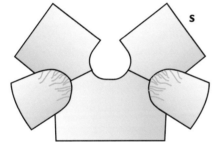

18 Cut two 4½in lengths of elastic and sew one piece to the bottom of each sleeve, on the wrong side, ¾in up from the hem; stretch the elastic as you sew so that it extends the entire width of the fabric, as you did for the legs of the bloomers. With right sides together, stitch the underarm seams (**t**).

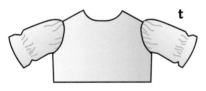

19 Take the 10 x 30in piece of skirt fabric you cut earlier and make a mark 1½in in on each side of the 30in length. Run a gathering stitch along the top of the skirt between these marks. Gather the top of the skirt so that it is the same width as the bodice and, with right sides together, sew the skirt to the bottom of the bodice. Zigzag the raw edge of this seam to prevent it from fraying.

20 Sew the back seam of the skirt using a ½in seam; start from the bottom, and leave a 4in opening up to the point where the skirt meets the bodice. To neaten the remaining raw edges, fold each side under ¼in twice and topstitch (**u**).

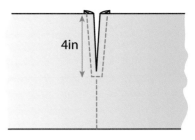

21 From the remaining dress fabric, cut a bias piece measuring 1½ x 8in; use this to make a length of double-fold bias binding. Use this to bind the neck of the bodice, folding under and finishing off the raw ends. Sew lace around the neck opening, then hem the bottom of the dress. Sew two snaps/poppers on the back opening of the dress, one at the top and one at the waist.

Congratulations: your doll is now ready to be dressed and presented as a gift, or sat in that special place for you to enjoy!

The finished dress from the back, showing the opening

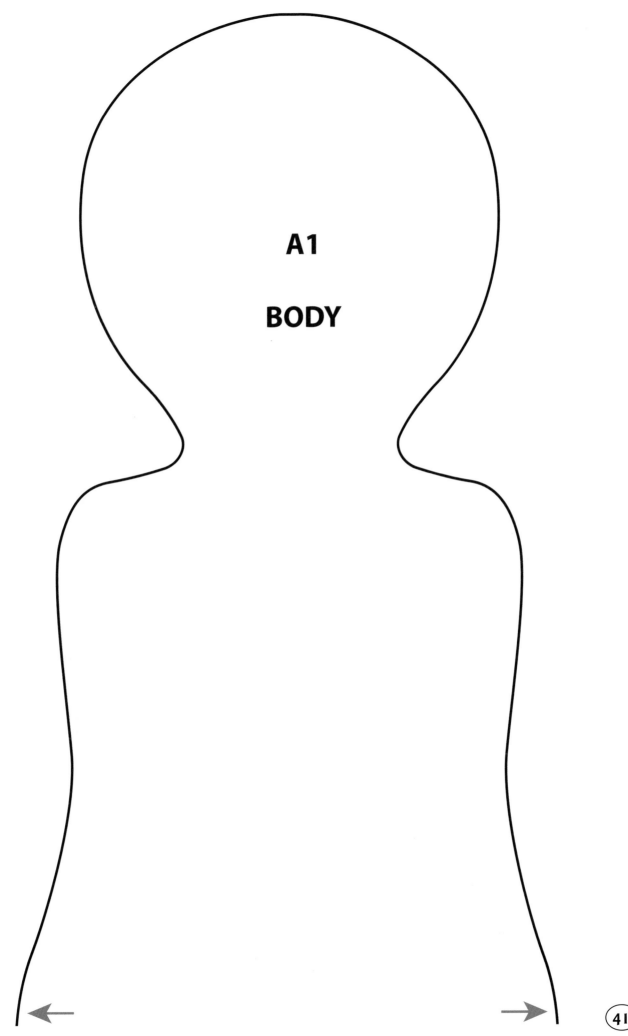

A1

BODY

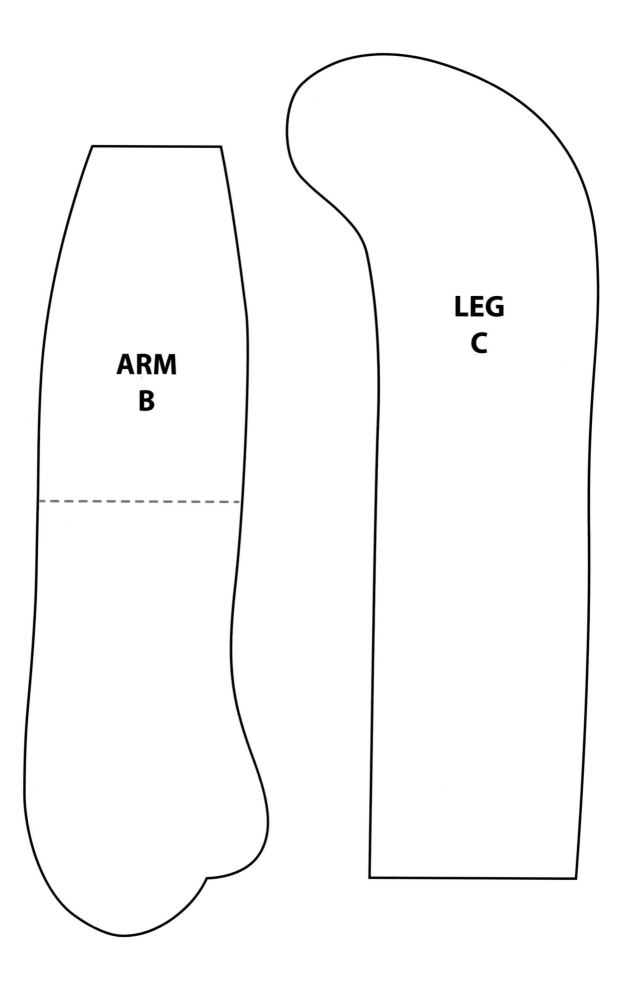

ARM
B

LEG
C

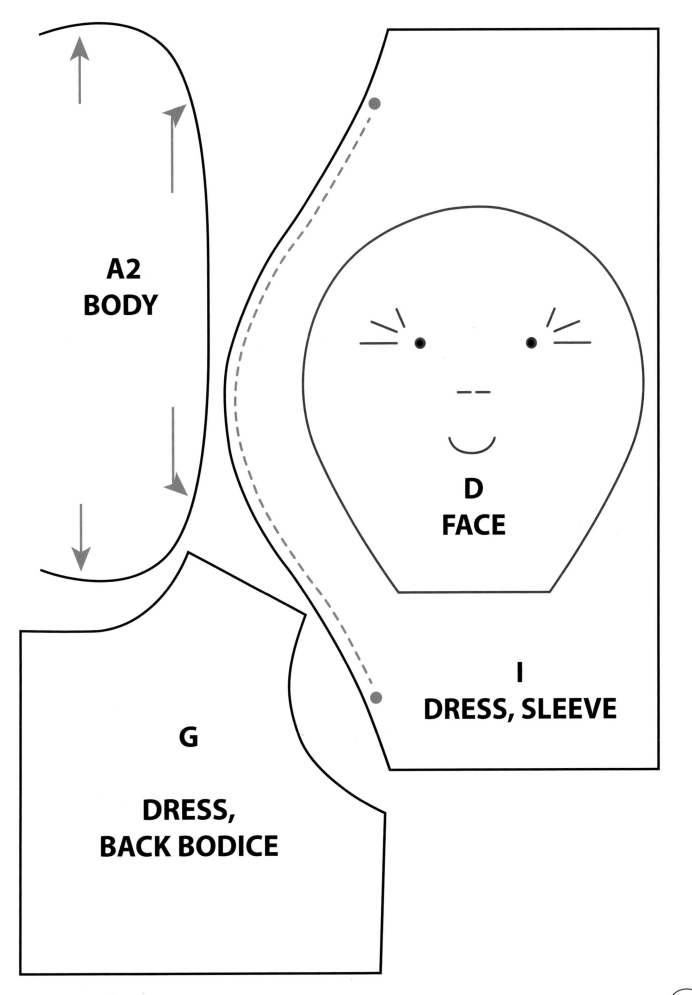

A2
BODY

D
FACE

I
DRESS, SLEEVE

G

DRESS,
BACK BODICE

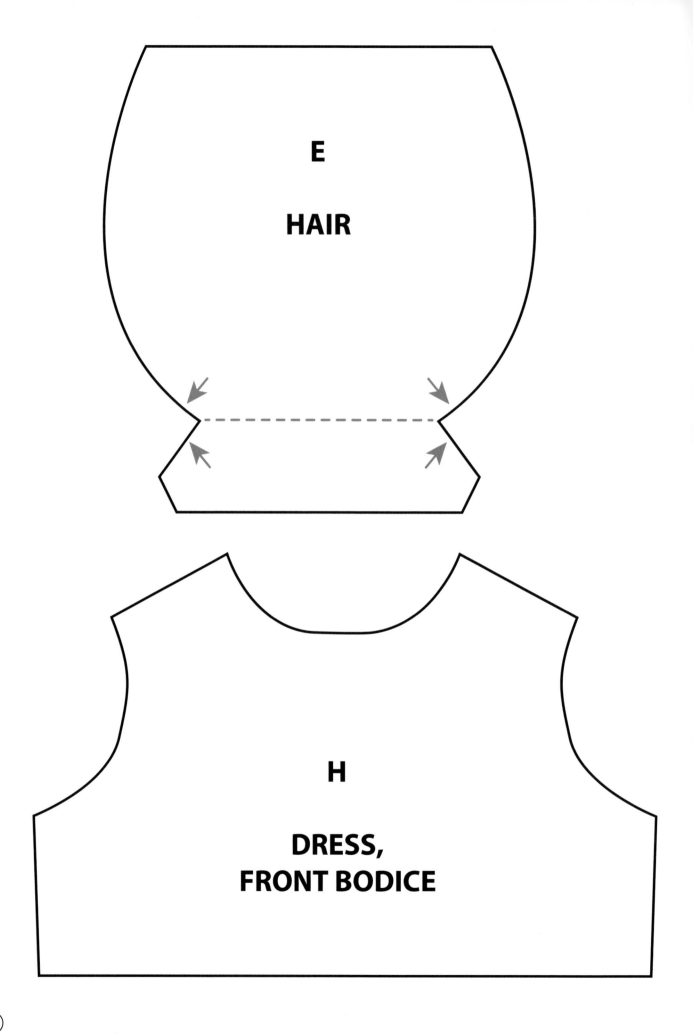

E

HAIR

H

DRESS,
FRONT BODICE

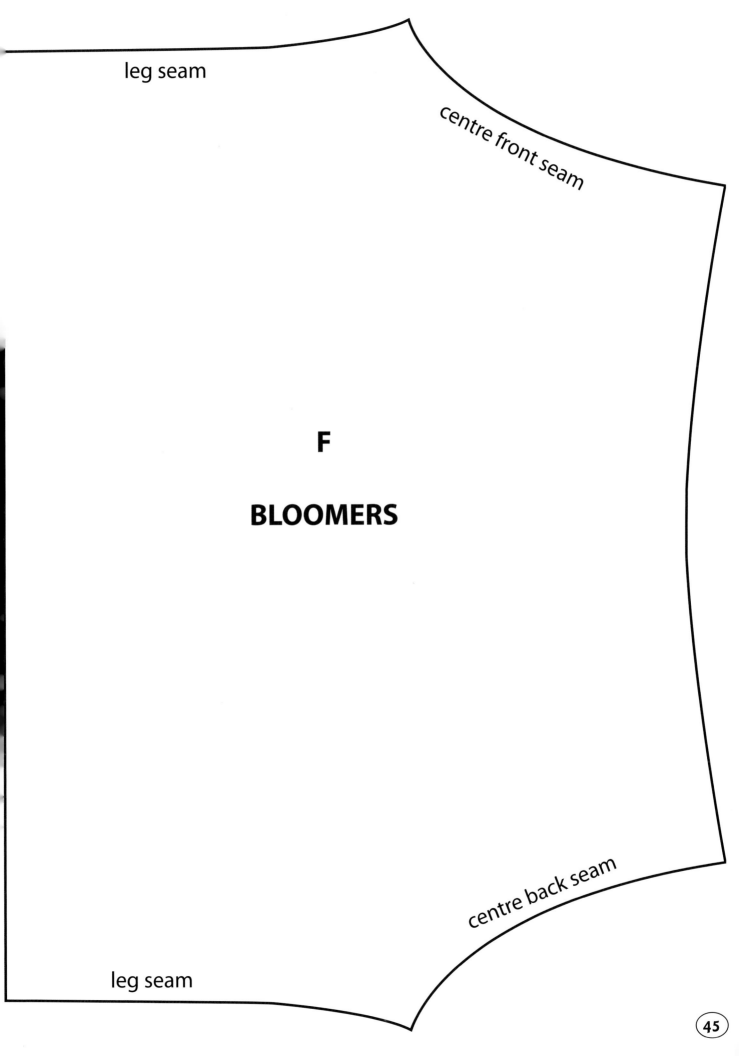

leg seam

centre front seam

F

BLOOMERS

centre back seam

leg seam

ROTARY CUTTING

Rotary cutting is one of the most time-saving skills you can learn, because it removes the need to mark and cut individual pieces of fabric. As a result, it speeds up piecing the quilt, and – if you use the method correctly – it will improve the accuracy of your piecing. Another great bonus is that you can cut several layers of fabric at a time; don't try and cut too many layers together, though, as the finished pieces will not be so accurate.

Rotary cutters look like pizza cutters, but the blades are razor-sharp! There are several types of rotary cutter available, featuring different-sized blades, various handle shapes, and the option of a protective guard for the blade. If you're new to rotary cutting, we suggest beginning with a medium-sized rotary cutter with a 45mm replaceable blade.

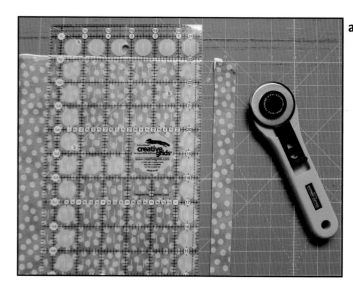

Preparing the fabric

Assuming that you are working with the full width of your fabric (normally 44in), fold the fabric in half lengthwise and match the selvedges. Place the fabric on the rotary cutting mat, and with the bulk of the fabric on your left (assuming you are right-handed), place a long quilters' ruler across the fabric, matching one of the horizontal line markings to the fold. Using a rotary cutting ruler, cut off just enough from the raw edge of the fabric to give a straight edge to measure from (**a**).

☞ REMEMBER

Always use a rotary cutter with the correct mat, and don't use an ordinary classroom or metal ruler: the cutters are very sharp, and can slip if not used with the right equipment.

Cutting strips

Turn the fabric (or board) around, so that the bulk of fabric is now on your right and the trimmed edge on the left. Always measure and cut from a trimmed edge, using the measurement marking on the ruler. To cut strips, align the appropriate measurement on your ruler with the left (trimmed) edge of the fabric. For example, to cut a 3in strip, place the 3in line of the edge of the fabric (**b**).

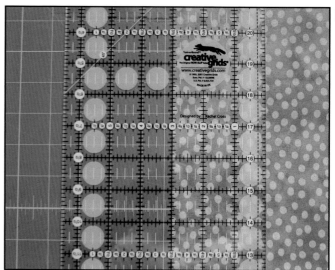

Place your left hand firmly on the ruler, and start to cut the fabric, starting at the bottom (nearest to you). For safety, always cut away from your body. As you cut up the fabric 'walk' your left-hand fingers up the ruler, maintaining pressure on it so that the fabric does not slip (**c**). While you are using the rotary cutter, ensure that you keep the fingers of your other hand well away from the blade. If the strip you need to cut is larger than your ruler (an 8in strip, for example), use the markings on the cutting board to measure the strip, then line up the ruler with the proper markings on the board to make your cut.

Cutting squares and rectangles

To cut individual squares, cut a strip to the required width and trim off the selvedge edges. Turn the strip around by 90° and, using the appropriate measurement on your ruler, measure from the left edge of the fabric and cut the squares (**d**).

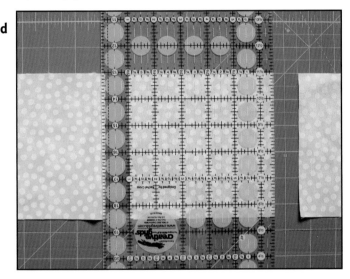

Use a similar method to cut rectangles; cut a strip to the size of the width of the rectangles first, and then sub-cut it into the length of the rectangles.

Cutting triangles

The easiest way to rotary-cut several right-angled triangles is to cut a square and then sub-cut the square into half-square or quarter-square triangles.

Half-square triangles

A half-square triangle is a right-angled triangle that has the bias grain of the fabric on the long side (**a**). You make a half-square triangle by cutting a square along one of the diagonals (**b**).

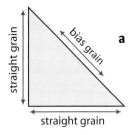

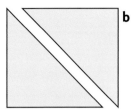

OK so far, you may say – but how do I work out the size of square that will give me a particular-sized triangle? Easy: the calculations for your square are based on the finished size of your half-square triangle unit (**c**). So, your first step is to work out your finished unit size. Then you add ⅞in. That's it: you simply add ⅞in to the required finished size of your half-square triangle unit.

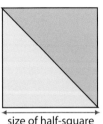

size of half-square triangle unit

So, for example, if you want a half-square triangle with finished short edges of 4in (so that you can join two of them to make a 4in square), you need to start with a 4⅞in square and cut it diagonally (**d**). If you stitch two of these half-square triangles together along the longest (bias) edge, you will make a square measuring 4½in (**e**) (ie finished size 4in).

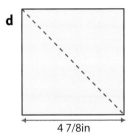

4 7/8in

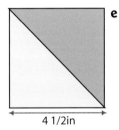

4 1/2in

Quarter-square triangles

A quarter-square triangle is a right-angled triangle that has the bias of the fabric on the two short sides (**a**). You make a quarter-square triangle by cutting a square along both diagonals (**b**). Once again, the calculations for the size of your original square are based on the finished size of the unit (**c**).

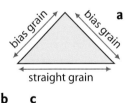

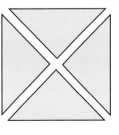

size of quarter-square triangle unit

So, your first step is to work out your finished unit size, then you add 1¼in.

So, for example, if you want a quarter-square triangle with finished long edges of 4in (so that you can join four of them to make a 4in square), you need to start with a 5¼in square and cut it diagonally in both directions. If you stitch two of these quarter-square triangles together along the short sides (the bias edges) you will make a half-square triangle measuring 4⅞in on the short sides (**d**). If you sew four of the quarter-square triangles together you will make a square measuring 4½in (**e**) (ie finished size 4in).

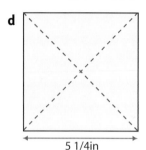 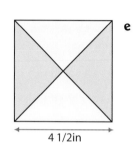

5 1/4in   4 1/2in

Quick-pieced half-square triangles

Here's an easy method to make two identical squares, each containing two half-square triangles, which means that you don't have to stitch a seam between bias edges.

1 From each fabric, cut a square ⅞in larger than the finished size of the stitched unit. Draw a diagonal line on the back of the lighter-coloured square, then draw stitching lines ¼in each side of the diagonal (**a**). Place this on top of the other patterned square, right sides together, and sew along the two stitching lines (**b**) (not the centre diagonal).

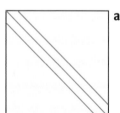 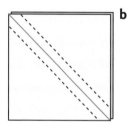

2 Use a rotary cutter to cut along the diagonal line (**c**), and open out each square (**d**). Press the seam allowances towards the darker fabric on each unit.

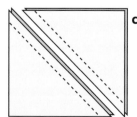 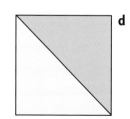

Multiple half-square triangles

1 To make several units at a time, draw a grid of squares on the back of the lighter-coloured fabric, where the squares are 1in bigger than the finished units (**a**).

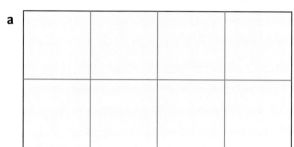

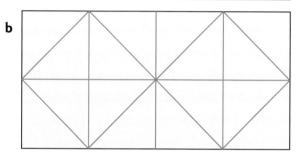

2 Draw diagonal lines on the grid as shown (**b**), then stitching lines ¼in either side of the diagonal lines (**c**).

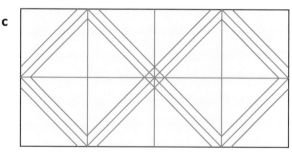

3 Sew along all the stitching lines (**d**). Cut along all the diagonal lines, and the horizontal and vertical lines of the grid (**e**).

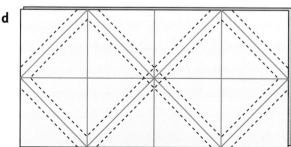

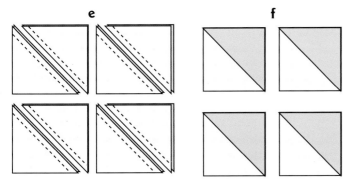

4 Open out the blocks and press them (**f**); trim them to size, making sure the diagonal line on your square ruler is lined up with the diagonal seam.

Quick-pieced quarter-square triangles

1 To make a square composed of four quarter-square triangles, firstly make two of the half-square triangle units as described above (**a**). Put the two pieces right sides together, alternating the colours (**b**), with the diagonal seams aligned and pressed in opposite directions.

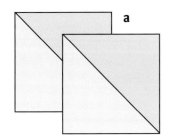 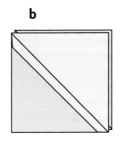

2 On the back of one of these units, draw another diagonal line, at right angles to the seam; draw a stitching line ¼in to each side of the diagonal (**c**).

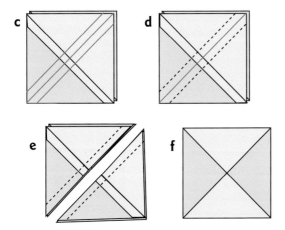

3 Sew along the stitching lines either side of the marked diagonal (**d**), then again cut them apart on the marked line (**e**). Open up the two triangles (**f**) and press the seams towards the darker fabric.

In these details you can see different ways of using pieced triangles

PIECING

Machine piecing

The normal seam allowance for quilt making is ¼in, and all the piecing measurements for projects in this book include this ¼in seam allowance. In order to sew a ¼in seam accurately with your sewing machine it is best to have a ¼in foot. If you do not, you can make a seam guide by using ¼in masking tape – stick a piece on the throat plate of your machine, ¼in to the right of the needle.

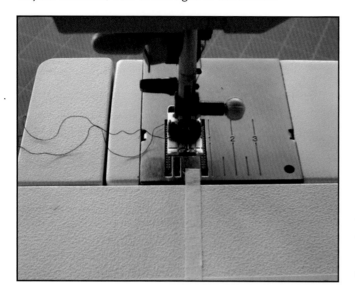

To machine piece, use a straight stitch and set the stitch length to 2 to 2.5. Place the two pieces of fabric to be joined right sides together and align the raw edges with the edge of your ¼in foot or the ¼in tape you have placed on your sewing machine throat plate. Before you start to join these

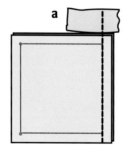

pieces, feed a small scrap of fabric under the needle and sew part-way through it, stopping just before the end of the scrap (**a**). Place the fabric pair in front of the presser foot and continue stitching (without lifting the presser foot or cutting the thread). This method of starting on a scrap of fabric will prevent threads and fabric from being caught in the foot plate.

As you sew the fabric pieces together, gently guide the fabric with your hands and check that it feeds through the machine evenly and without slipping. If you want to pin pieces together before you sew, then make sure the pins are at right angles to the sewing line, and remove the pins just before you reach them.

Chain piecing

Chain piecing is a quick way to sew several units in succession and also has the added advantage of saving thread. Feed the pieces under the presser foot, one after another (**a**), with a few stitches in between (without cutting the threads or lifting the foot), and then cut them apart when the chain is complete. Finish the chain by sewing onto a pice of scrap fabric, ready to start the next chain.

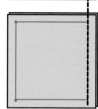

Hand piecing

All the projects in this book can be made without the use of a sewing machine. If you are hand piecing the projects you must measure and mark the seam allowances on all the pieces before you sew. To do this, use a ruler with a ¼in marking, and a pencil. (You don't need to worry whether you can erase the pencil marks, as you will be marking on the wrong sides of the fabric.)

To hand piece, place the two pieces of fabric to be joined right sides together; pin through and match the corners and along the stitching lines, placing the pins at right angles to the sewing line (**a**).

Use a single strand of cotton thread. Backstitch to secure the thread in the fabric (avoid knots, as these create bumps, and can also become unravelled), and sew with small, even running stitches along the marked sewing lines (**b**). Finish your seam with another backstitch and trim the thread – don't sew into the seam allowance. If you have to stitch over seams, then make a backstitch each side of the overlap to reinforce the seam.

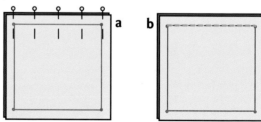

Pressing

It is important to press your work as it progresses, especially if you are piecing by machine because it will then move under the presser foot easily.

Press your work by placing the iron up and down on the fabric rather than sliding it over the pieces. Start pressing with a dry iron – use steam with caution as this can distort the fabric.

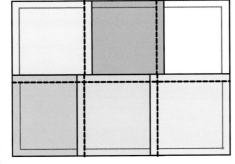

As a general rule, press seams towards the dark fabric, but at intersections (eg when joining rows together), press seams in the opposite directions as shown here; this helps opposing seams to butt up together, which will help to produce a flat join and reduce bulk.

Squaring up a block

Once you've pieced a block, it's important to square it up before you join it to other blocks or sashing; this process removes any slight inaccuracies or distortions that have crept in during the piecing.

1 When you're squaring up a block, you always square two adjacent edges at a time. So start by placing the block on the cutting mat with the two sides you want to square first to the bottom and the right. Lay the ruler over the block, with the correct block measurement in the bottom left corner of the block. (For example: if you want to make a block 6½in square, then the 6½in measurement should be in the top left corner.) Adjust the ruler over the block until you judge that the block is centred and the edges of the block go slightly over the upper left corner measurement (**a**).

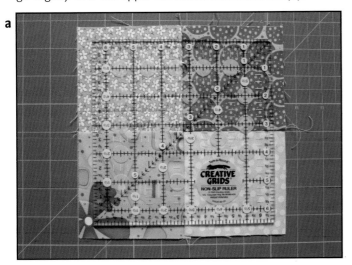

2 Using the rotary cutter, trim the right side of the block and then the bottom of the block (**b**); now the bottom right corner will be perfectly square.

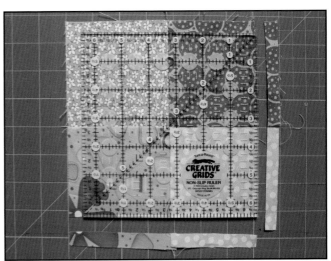

3 Carefully turn the block round (or move your mat). Lay the ruler over the block again, with the correct block measurement in the top left corner of the block, and match this up exactly to the corner and the two straight edges you have just trimmed, as shown (**c**). The other two edges (untrimmed) are now in the bottom right corner. Cut the right side and the bottom edge as before (**d**); you will now have a perfectly square 6½in block.

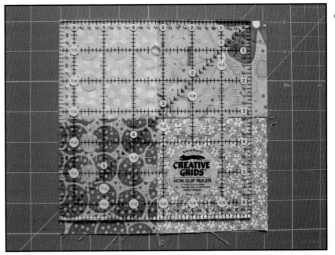

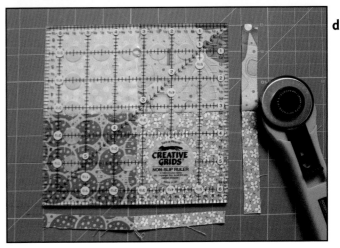

Squaring up a half-square triangle block

1 If you are squaring up a unit made of two half-square triangles, it is important to use the diagonal line (45° angle) on your ruler/setting square. In the photographs below, we show the sequence for trimming a block down to 4in square. Before you trim any of the sides, lay the ruler on top of the block, aligning the diagonal line with the diagonal seam, so that the edges of the block go slightly over the 4in measurements in all directions (**a**).

2 Trim the top and right-hand edges as shown (**b**), then turn the block around 180° so that the trimmed edges are exactly on the 4in measurements and the untrimmed edges appear beyond the ruler (**c**).

3 Trim the top and right-hand edges as before (**d**); you now have an accurate 4in square, with the diagonal going across it at a perfect 45° angle.

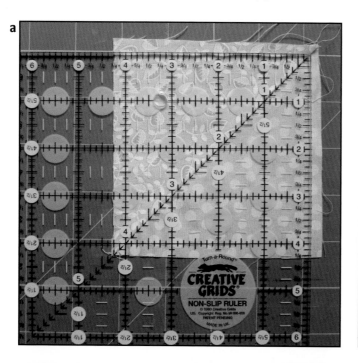

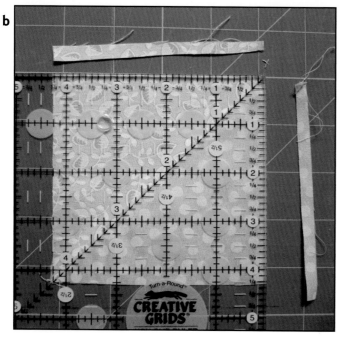

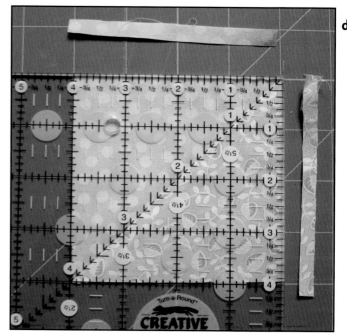

The word appliqué comes from the French, meaning 'application'; in quilting it means applying one piece of fabric onto a background fabric. There are several methods of appliqué, but in this book we've only used two – needle-turn appliqué (for *Piggy in the Middle* and *Petals and Pinwheels*) and fusible-web appliqué (*ABC Quilt*). If you find that you enjoy appliqué, there are many patterns and books available which will give you the opportunity to expand your skills.

Needle-turn appliqué

In this method, fabric shapes are cut out with a seam allowance and then applied to the background using hand stitching. The name 'needle-turn' derives from the fact that the seam allowance on the shape is turned under with the point of the needle as you work.

The ABC quilt uses fusible web appliqué, with the edges of the patches decorated with blanket stitch embroidery

Fusible web appliqué

In this method, fusible webbing is used to adhere the shapes to the background fabric; you can then use hand or machine stitching to secure the pieces and add a decorative edge.

It's important to note that, when you're using fusible web for raw-edge appliqué projects, any asymmetrical templates must be reversed (as you work on the back of the fabric) – you'll see that for the ABC quilt (see page 12) the templates are drawn in reverse. (If you wanted to needle-turn a project like this, you would need to re-draw the templates the correct way around, as for that technique you work on the front of the appliqué fabric – and vice versa!)

Appliqué basics

Preparing the background

You should always cut the background fabric slightly larger than the finished requirement: add at least an inch to both the length and the width. This is because the process of appliquéing pieces onto the background can pull the fabric up a little. Also, if you spend a long time working on a piece of appliqué, sometimes the edges of the background can begin to fray; once you have finished appliquéing the shapes you can cut the background to size and have nice clean edges.

Transferring the pattern to the background

To begin with you must find the centre of the background fabric. To do this, fold the fabric in half lengthways and widthways, and finger-press the folds. The point where the folds cross is the centre of the background fabric; mark this with a pin, a pencil, or a dot of chalk.

There are several ways to transfer the pattern to your background fabric. The two we recommend are: tracing the pattern directly onto the background fabric, and using an overlay.

• Tracing the pattern onto the background

Either use a lightbox or tape the pattern to a window on a sunny day, and centre the background fabric, right side up, over the pattern and secure it. (If you're using a window, tape down both the pattern and the background fabric.) Then trace the pattern onto the background fabric using a water-soluble pen or quilting pencil.

• Using an overlay

This method is particularly useful if you are using a dark background fabric and it's difficult to trace through. For this method the pattern is traced onto a transparent or translucent material and placed over the background fabric, lining up the centre points; each appliqué piece is then positioned between the overlay and the background, using the traced design as a guide. Clear plastic sheets work well for the overlay, and so does thin, non-woven interfacing. If you are using the interfacing, you can tack/baste the overlay to the top of the background and then flip it down and up as you position each appliqué shape.

Needle-turn appliqué method

Preparation

For needle-turn appliqué, the appliqué shapes are cut out of fabric using either templates (plastic, cardboard or otherwise), or by pattern tracing (tracing paper, freezer paper, etc).

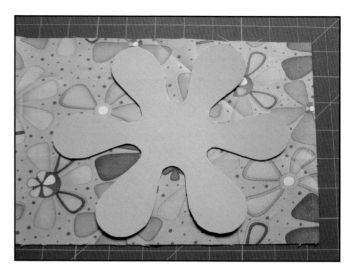

• Using templates

Create the template by tracing the relevant pattern pieces onto template plastic and cutting them out along the marked lines. Or, if you prefer to use card for your templates: trace or photocopy the shapes onto paper, stick the paper onto thin card, and cut out the template. Position each template on the right side of the appliqué fabric and trace around it using a water-soluble pen or a quilting pencil (**a**).

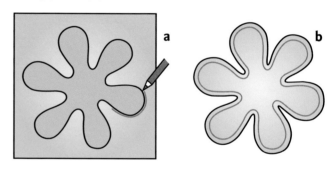

Cut out the shape, leaving a ⅛-¼in turning allowance around each shape (**b**). If you're a beginner, you'll find it easier to handle the appliqué pieces if they have the larger turning allowance, but this can create bulkiness on the underside of your appliqué. For this reason, cut as small a turning allowance as you find you can manipulate – don't make it too small, though, otherwise the stitches may pull out around corners.

• Using freezer paper

Trace each pattern piece onto the paper (matt) side of the freezer paper (**a**) and cut the shape out along the marked line (**b**). With a dry iron, press the freezer paper shape onto the right side of the fabric, shiny side down (**c**).

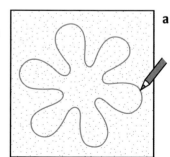

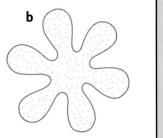

b

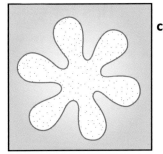

c

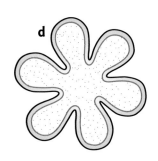

d

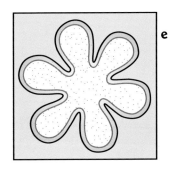

e

Trace around the shape with either a water-soluble pen or quilting pencil, and cut out the shape, again leaving a ⅛-¼in turning allowance as above (**d**). Remove the freezer paper, and appliqué the piece in position.

(If you prefer, instead of tracing around the shape and removing the freezer paper, you can appliqué the piece onto the background with the freezer paper still in place as shown in diagram **e**, folding under the edge as you go and removing the paper when you have finished.)

Additionally, you can use the freezer paper shape on the inside of your appliqué piece. To use this method, first of all pin the freezer paper, shiny side up, to the wrong side of the fabric and cut out with a seam allowance as above. Then fold the seam allowances around the freezer paper, ironing as you go – the fabric will adhere to the freezer paper. Be careful only to iron the seam allowance; don't let the iron come into contact with the shiny side of the freezer paper.

☆ HINT

Whichever method you choose, trace and cut the appliqué pieces on the bias of the fabric; this will make it much easier to turn under the spare fabric, and your appliqué shapes will be much less likely to fray.

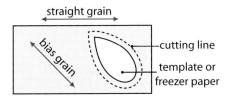

Once all the edges are folded under, sew the appliqué patch to the background fabric, leaving the freezer paper shape in place inside the patch as you stitch. After you have stitched all the way around, you will need to cut a slit in the back of the background fabric, behind the appliqué piece, in order to pull out the freezer paper shape.

Here are some pointers you'll find useful as you get ready to appliqué:

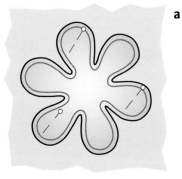

a

- Choose threads that match the appliqué fabric, not the background. If you can't match the appliqué fabric directly, use a shade lighter than the fabric as darker threads are harder to hide.

- Use at least two pins on each appliqué patch to ensure that it can't move out of place as you stitch (**a**).

☆ HINT

Appliqué pins are easier to use than normal sewing pins, as they are shorter and not so cumbersome.

- Always begin your appliqué by sewing any underlying pieces first – that is, any patch that is overlapped by another (**b**). Begin on a straight portion of the piece if possible, not on a point or corner. When you are matching two pieces together or overlapping one piece on another, start about an inch behind where two pieces meet or overlap.

- On pattern pieces with inside curves, clip a small amount into the seam allowance so that the fabric will 'give' a little when it's turned under (**c**).

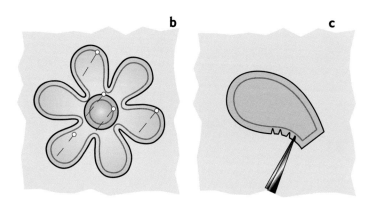

b

c

Stitching

1 Position an appliqué piece on the background and secure with pins.

2 Knot the thread and pull the needle up through the back of the appliqué piece on your drawn line or at the edge of your freezer paper. This will be the edge of the appliqué when the fabric is turned under so that the knot will be hidden inside the fabric (**a**).

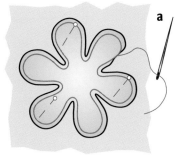

☞ REMEMBER

Begin stitching on a straight or gently curved edge, not a point or corner.

3 Take the needle back down through the background fabric exactly opposite the stitch on the appliqué shape (**b**), making sure that the stitch isn't slanting either forwards or backwards. Bringing the needle up from the wrong side, take a stitch through the background fabric and the edge of the appliqué piece, catching only a couple of threads of the appliqué fabric (**c**). Keep the stitches small, allowing about 1/8in between stitches. The thread will be visible on the wrong side of your work and almost invisible on the right side.

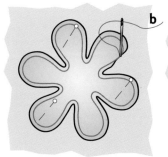
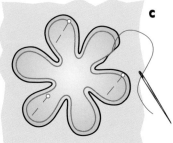

4 Continue stitching around the edge of the appliqué shape, turning under the seam allowance with the point of the needle as you work, and following the drawn line on the right side of the fabric (**d**).

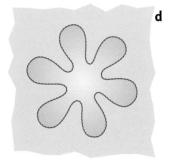

Extra tips for great appliqué

Some people find sewing particular appliqué shapes frustrating, but if you follow the hints below you'll find that you can easily tame them!

• Curves

On some inner curves you might find that your fabric pulls and will not turn under easily. In this case make small clips along the curve as shown, from the outside edge halfway to the sewing line as needed. Outside curves should not need clipping; however, if you find that they are too bulky, trim the seam allowance slightly so that any fullness fits under the turned edge.

• Outer points

To make sharp outer points, sew the appliqué piece right up to the point, with the last stitch coming directly out of the point. If the point is a 90° angle or more (**a**), simply needle-turn the fabric on the other side of the point under. Pull gently on the thread to make sure that the point is realigned after turning, and continue sewing (**b**).

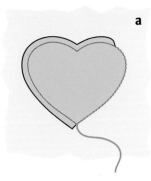
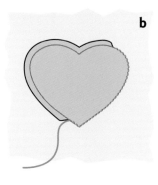

If the angle is sharper (less than 90°) it is useful to remove some of the extra fabric in the seam allowance before continuing. To do this, fold the seam under and clip off any extra fabric that shows behind appliqué piece (**c**). Then, turn the point in two stages: first, fold the fabric downwards so that you can access the inside of the appliqué patch, and fold the fabric point up inside the shape to create a 'dog ear' (**d**). Replace the appliqué patch flat against the background, and again pull gently on the thread to make sure that the point is fully

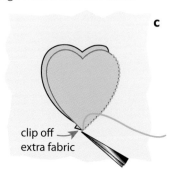

clip off extra fabric

'out.' Fold under the fabric that is on the other side of the point and continue sewing (**e**). If you want to accentuate the point even more, you can make the stitch that comes out of the point a slight bit longer.

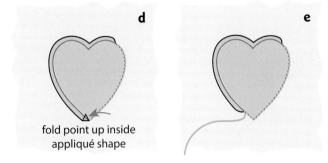

fold point up inside
appliqué shape

• Inner points

Before you sew, mark a line on your appliqué piece from the outside edge of the fabric to the centre of your inner point (**a**). Sew to within a couple of stitches of the inner point (**b**), making your stitches closer to each other up to this point. Clip the fabric on the drawn line, almost all the

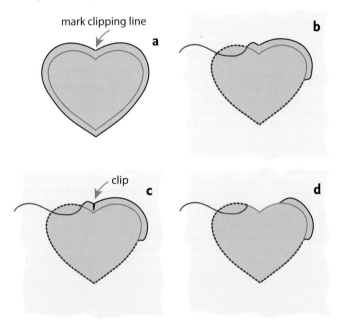

mark clipping line

a

b

clip

c

d

way, but not quite to the appliqué line or template (**c**). Fold the seam allowance under up to the clipped point, then fold under the 'uphill' side of the appliqué piece that is just past the inner point (**d**). Make the first stitch in the centre of the inner point only through the appliqué piece, not the background (which will help secure any fraying edges); then make the second stitch through the appliqué piece and into the background. Open out the 'uphill' side of the appliqué piece and continue sewing (**e**).

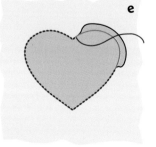

e

For inner points that are more than a curve but not quite as sharp as a V shape (more like a tight U), make a 'crow's foot' clip (three small snips together) in the centre as shown, but only clip two thirds of the way to the line or template.

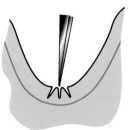

• Circles

For great circles, make a template of your finished circle size using thin card (**a**). Cut a circle from your appliqué fabric quite a bit larger than the card. Place your fabric over your card (**b**), then work large running stitches around edge of your fabric behind the card (**c**) and pull up the gathering

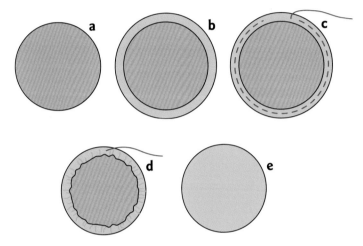

a

b

c

d

e

stitches (**d**). On the right side of the fabric, press the circle flat with a hot iron, but without steam. Once the shape is cool, loosen the gathering stitches carefully and remove the card. (You can trim the seam before stitching if it turns out to be too bulky.) You should now have a perfect circle (**e**) ready to appliqué on your project.

Fusible web appliqué method

Preparation

For fusible web appliqué, the pattern pieces are traced onto the shiny (paper) side of the fusible web; the shape is then roughly cut out and ironed on to the reverse side of the appliqué fabric. For appliqué projects that will be secured by hand or machine stitch around the edges, it is best to use a lightweight fusible webbing as it is tricky to get a needle (hand or machine) through the heavyweight versions; read the directions on the product you plan to use beforehand, as specific products and uses may differ. In general, fusible web has a smooth side and a rough side; the smooth side is the paper that is used to protect the iron-on webbing, and the rough side is the adhesive.

Doing the appliqué

1 Trace the appliqué patterns directly onto the paper side of the fusible webbing. (Remember: when you're using fusible web, the design needs to be reversed from the final way you want it to appear.) Roughly cut out the shape (**a**)

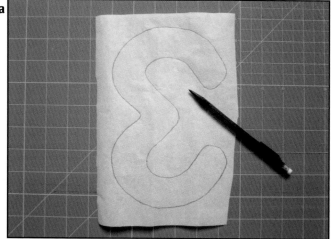

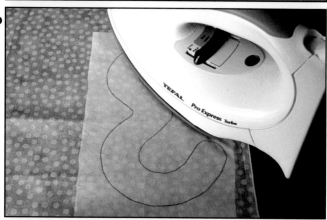

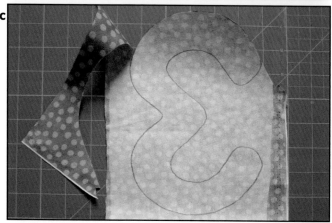

– do not cut directly on the lines at this stage. Then, iron these pieces onto the reverse side of the appropriate appliqué fabric (**b**); after the fabric has cooled, cut the appliqué pieces out on the drawn lines (**c**). (The patterns are rough-cut prior to ironing on to the fabric, then cut out precisely afterwards, to ensure that the fabric patches have the adhesive all the way out to the edges.)

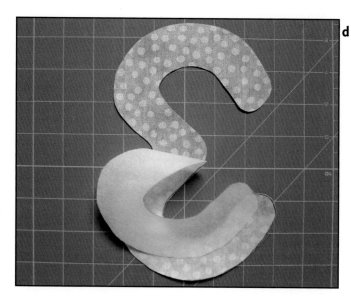

2 Iron the background fabric before fusing to make sure there are no wrinkles or creases. Remove the backing paper from the appliqué shapes (**d**), then, with the adhesive side down, place your appliqué shapes on the right side of the background fabric and press them into place.

☆ HINT

Fuse the shapes in place by pressing up and down with the iron, rather than by moving it back and forth or in a circular motion, to ensure that the appliqué patch doesn't move out of position while you're fusing.

3 After all the appliqué pieces have been ironed onto the background, sew around the edges of each patch either by machine or by hand (**e**), using any type of decorative stitch.

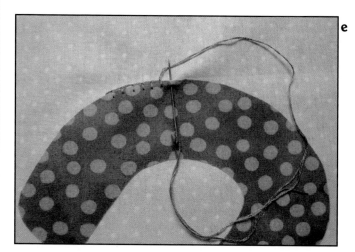

Layering, marking and tacking/basting

There are many different products on the market which you can use for marking out your quilting design. The marking method you choose will often depend on the colour(s) of the quilt top; you need to be able to see the quilting design clearly against the different fabrics. On light fabric, for example, use an ordinary pencil, a blue wash-out pen (the marks are removed with a light dab of clean water once the quilting is complete), or a purple evaporating pen (the marks disappear within about 24 hours). On dark fabric, use a white, silver or yellow pencil, a white marking pen, or chalk.

1 Press the quilt top first, and then mark your chosen quilting lines and patterns on the right side.

 REMEMBER

If you mark your quilting lines with a wash-away pen, then don't iron over these lines – they will become permanent!

2 Cut a piece of wadding 3-4in larger than the quilt top; aim to have approximately 2in of wadding showing around the quilt top on all sides. Cut the backing to the same size as the wadding.

3 Lay the backing fabric right side down onto a flat surface – a large table or the floor. Keep this fabric as taut as possible, but do not stretch it: masking tape or soft furnishing clamps help to keep it in place. Lay the wadding on top, smoothing out any wrinkles with your hand, and working from the centre so that any excess wadding goes over the edges of the backing fabric.

REMEMBER

Do not press the wadding directly with an iron, especially if it contains polyester – it will melt!

4 Centre the quilt top over the backing and wadding to make the final layer of the sandwich. Starting at the centre and working towards the edges, smooth out any wrinkles in the top.

5 Using a long needle and contrasting thread, tack/baste the three layers of the quilt 'sandwich' together with large running stitches. Start from the centre of the quilt,

and smooth the top and wadding as you baste – also check that the backing stays as flat as possible. Baste horizontally across the whole quilt, with rows of stitches about 2in apart; repeat with vertical stitches (**a**).

a

There are various other methods you can use to baste the layers of your quilt sandwich. One way is by using safety pins (the curved ones are easier to use), and this is a good idea if you are machine quilting. Keep the basting pins 6-8in apart (**b**).

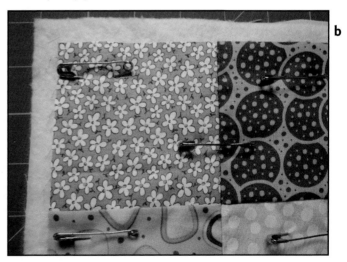

b

Other basting options include:

- a basting 'gun' which secures the layers together with small plastic ties
- basting spray which temporarily bonds the layers together
- fusible wadding

Remove the basting stitches, pins or plastic ties once the quilting is complete.

Quilting

Quilting is the stitching that holds the three layers of a quilt together, but it also adds decoration and enhances the piecing in the blocks. Whether you are quilting by hand or machine, always begin quilting in the centre of the quilt and work outwards; this way the quilt stays nice and flat, and you avoid any puckers in the centre.

Quilting by hand

If you're using a frame, secure the work in it so that it is firm but not taut – you need to be able to 'rock the needle' through all three layers (see below). Using a single strand of quilting thread (18-24in long), make a knot in the end. Working from the back, insert the needle about 1in away from where you want to begin quilting. Run the needle through the wadding and bring it through to the front of the work at the start point. Give the thread a gentle tug, to pull the knot into the wadding (**a**).

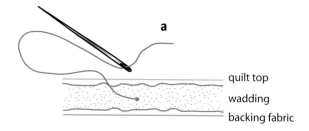

a

quilt top
wadding
backing fabric

The quilting stitch is a small running stitch which goes through all three layers – the quilt top, the wadding and the backing. Using a rocking motion with the needle, in and out of the work, aim to make three or four stitches (**b**) before you pull the thread through (**c**).

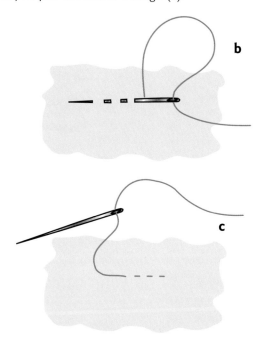

b

c

'In the ditch' quilting means that you sew along the seam line, and the stitches are less obvious than on other parts of the fabric patch. Don't try to quilt through folded seams as the bulk will make it difficult to push the needle through. If you quilt at least ¼in away from a seam then you should avoid the bulk of folded seam allowances. When you are getting near to the end of the thread, or if you want to finish quilting, tie a knot in the thread close to the quilt top, and take the needle into the work right beside the thread. Pull this knot into the wadding. Bring the needle up

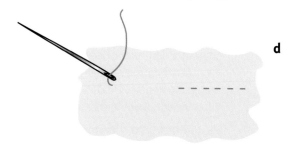

d

about an inch from where the quilting finished (**d**) and cut off the excess thread. The photograph below shows an example of hand quilting.

Quilting by machine

Although machine quilting is quicker than hand quilting, it takes a lot of practice to achieve good results. If you're a beginner, start with sewing straight lines only, and leave curves and free-motion quilting until you have more experience! For example, if you wanted to machine quilt the first project (*Baby Charms*, see page 8) using straight lines of machining instead of the curved design that we've used, you could sew on the diagonal across the squares, and then quilt in the ditch along the border seams. You can also use fancy machine stitches for quilting if you wish. It is important to use a walking foot on your machine when

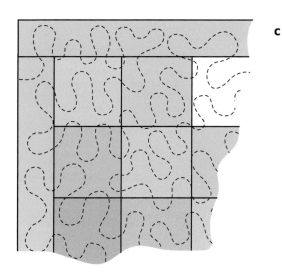

c

quilting, as shown above – this attachment moves the top and bottom fabrics at the same rate, and so helps to prevent folds and puckers being formed in the backing fabric as the quilt moves under the machine.

You can achieve more decorative quilting if you drop the 'feed dogs' on your machine. (These are the little ridged areas under the needle which move the fabric along at a regular speed.) Dropping the feed dogs allows you to stitch curves (**a**), and to create simple stipple or vermicelli quilting (**b** and **c**) – but if you're new to quilting, practise on spare fabric and wadding before you try the effect on your quilt.

Once you're a bit more confident, you can create even more sophisticated designs with this kind of free machine quilting; make up some spare quilt 'sandwiches' with offcuts of fabric and wadding, and try producing simple flowers, leaf and heart shapes.

REMEMBER

Always put a fresh needle in your machine when you start to quilt; use a 70/10 or 70/11.

If you have enjoyed making the quilt top, but don't want to tackle the quilting, then your work can be professionally quilted using a long-arm machine (**d**).

a

b
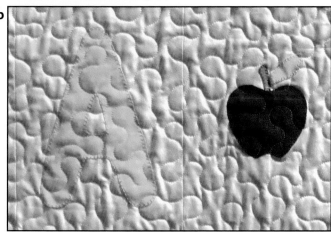

d

Binding is the strip of fabric that's used to cover the raw edges of a quilt after it's quilted, and it is one of the last steps before you can finally say that the quilt is finished. Binding can be made from a fabric that is already in the quilt or you can choose something new. We suggest cutting the binding strips 2½in wide – after folding and attaching this gives a finished binding width of about ½in.

You can make your finished binding wider if you prefer, but as well as cutting your strips wider accordingly, you'll also need to attach the binding more than ¼in from the edge of the quilt, to make sure that you have enough quilt edge to 'fill' your binding once it is folded over. (You'll also need a larger amount of binding fabric if you do this, don't forget.) If your pattern has patchwork going right out to the edge of the quilt, without any border, you won't want to make the finished binding any wider than ¼in as otherwise it would cover some of your pieced design.

☞ REMEMBER

Join the binding onto the quilt top before you trim away the excess wadding and backing; it's much easier to attach the binding this way, as otherwise the layers can move in relation to each other.

You need to cut enough strips to go all the way round the quilt, plus 6-8in overlap. Cut the strips on the straight grain of the fabric, and where possible across the full width of the fabric (approximately 44in) to minimise the number of joins. So, for example, if the quilt measures 36in square you will need to cut four strips across the width of the fabric. The binding is usually attached as one long strip to avoid bulky seams at the corners, and to enable you to make attractive mitred corners.

This binding shows a diagonal join in the fabric strips

1 To create one long strip of binding fabric, join the ends of the strips using a diagonal seam. Lay the first binding strip right side up, and position the end of a second strip on top, right sides together and at a 90° angle (**a**). Mark a diagonal line from upper left to lower right and stitch along the line (**b**). Trim the excess fabric to ¼in away from the seam (**c**) and press the seam open (**d**), then add the other strips of binding fabric in the same way.

2 Fold and press the binding strip in half lengthways, with the wrong sides of fabric together (**e**).

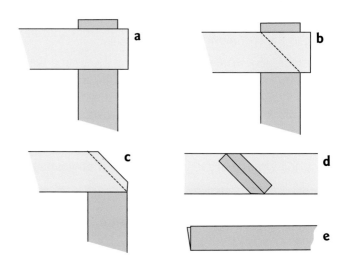

☞ REMEMBER

For this technique you fold the fabric wrong sides together.

Starting approximately half-way along one of the sides of the quilt, align the raw edge of the binding with the edge of the quilt top. Leaving a free 'tail' of binding roughly 6in long, stitch through all layers, using a ¼in seam and stopping the stitching ¼in from the corner of the quilt (**f**). (If you are using a wider seam allowance, end the seam the same distance from the approaching quilt edge as the width of the seam allowance.) Backstitch at this point and cut the threads.

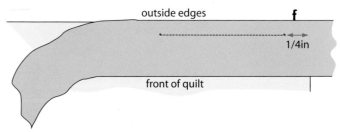

3 Turn the quilt around to the next edge. To mitre the corner of the binding, fold the binding strip straight up at 90° to the edge you have just sewn (**g**); this creates a diagonal fold of binding in the corner. Finger-press this fold, and then bring the unsewn binding strip back down over itself, lining up the raw edges again (**h**). Begin stitching again, starting right at the folded edge of the binding and still using a ¼in seam.

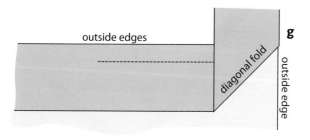

outside edges | diagonal fold | outside edge | **g**

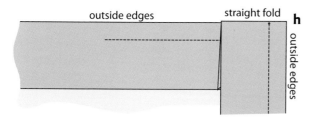

outside edges | straight fold | outside edges | **h**

4 Continue sewing the binding around the quilt, mitring each corner as before. Stop stitching roughly 6in before the beginning of your original stitching line.

5 Lay the first free tail of the binding strip flat along the edge of the quilt top, then lay the other free end on top of it; carefully trim the binding strip so this overlap is the same width as the binding (**i**) – normally 2½in.

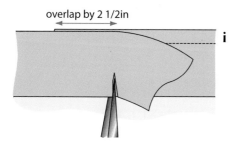

overlap by 2 1/2in | **i**

6 Unfold both ends of the binding strip and place them right sides together at 90°, as you did when joining the original binding strips. Mark a diagonal line as before, and then sew across this diagonal. Check that the binding fits correctly, repositioning and resewing the overlap if necessary. Then trim the excess, refold the binding in half, match it to the edge of the quilt top and stitch it in place (**j**).

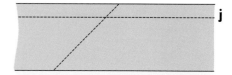

j

7 Trim the wadding and backing level with the raw edges of the quilt top and binding.

8 Fold the binding to the back of the quilt, covering the machine stitching, and blindstitch it in place. The mitres should fold neatly at the corners to form a 45° angle on the front and the back (**k**).

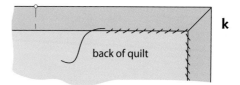

back of quilt | **k**

PUDDLEDUCKS, in Sevenoaks, is well-established as a quilt shop in the south east. You will also see us at many of the quilting shows around the country, including Quilts UK at Malvern, and the Festival of Quilts at the NEC. If you can't visit us in person, many of our wonderful fabrics are available to buy online; just have a browse through our website.

Puddleducks also offers a long-arm quilting service; if you love piecing, but find the thought of quilting your project daunting, long-arm quilting may be the ideal solution!

Puddleducks
116 St John's Hill
Sevenoaks
Kent TN13 3PD

telephone 01732 743642

website www.puddleducksquilts.co.uk